IF WITH
ALL
YOUR
HEART

OTHER BOOKS BY RICHARD W. O'FFILL

Expect Great Things
Transforming Prayer
Lord, Keep Your Mansions—Just Save My Children
Standing Firm

To order, call 1-800-765-6955.

Visit us at www.reviewandherald.com for information on other Review and Herald® products.

If you would like to communicate with the author directly, please visit his Web site: www.revivalsermons.org.

IF WITH
ALL YOUR HEART

A GOD-SEEKER'S GUIDE TO EFFECTIVE PRAYER

RICHARD W. O'FFILL

REVIEW AND HERALD® PUBLISHING ASSOCIATION
HAGERSTOWN, MD 21740

The author assumes full responsibility for the accuracy of all facts and quotations as cited in this book.

Texts credited to NKJV are from the New King James Version. Copyright © 1979, 1980, 1982 by Thomas Nelson, Inc. Used by permission. All rights reserved.

Texts credited to RSV are from the Revised Standard Version of the Bible, copyright © 1946, 1952, 1971, by the Division of Christian Education of the National Council of the Churches of Christ in the U.S.A. Used by permission.

This book was
Edited by Andy Nash
Copyedited by Jocelyn Fay and James Cavil
Designed by Willie S. Duke/Leumas Design
Cover photos by Getty Images
Typeset: 12/15 Bembo

PRINTED IN U.S.A.

08 07 06 05 04   5 4 3 2 1

R&H Cataloging Service
O'Ffill, Richard Wesley, 1940-
    If with all your heart: a God-seeker's guide to effective prayer.

    1. Prayer.   I. Title

242

ISBN 0-8280-1784-0

This book is dedicated to my wife, Betty,

who is my best friend and prayer partner.

*"Ye shall seek me, and
find me, when ye shall search for
me with all your heart."*
—Jeremiah 29:13.

CONTENTS

CHAPTER 1
A Matter of Life and Death 9

CHAPTER 2
Wheelin' and Dealin' Prayer 17

CHAPTER 3
If God Already Knows, Why Pray? . . 24

CHAPTER 4
Telling It Like It Is 30

CHAPTER 5
I'd Rather Not, But 37

CHAPTER 6
When No Is Really Yes 44

CHAPTER 7
An Ounce of Prevention 51

CHAPTER 8
How to Short-circuit Your Prayers . . . 59

CHAPTER 9
Say, "Pretty Please" 67

CHAPTER 10
Shall We Expect a Miracle? 75

CHAPTER 11
The Devil Made Me Do It 84

CHAPTER 12
Does It Help to Fast? 93

CHAPTER 13
Can Prayer Make You Rich? 99

CHAPTER 14
Strength in Numbers 107

CHAPTER 15
Bite-sized Faith 115

CHAPTER 16
Trust and Obey 122

CHAPTER 17
Prayer as a Lifestyle 129

A MATTER OF LIFE AND DEATH

hile it can be said that nobody will be saved merely because they pray, no one will be saved *unless* they pray. One person may never have heard a sermon because they were in some remote place where the gospel was never preached. Another person may never have read the Bible, either because they couldn't read or because there was not one available. Yet each of these people may be saved, because our Lord said, "Ask, and it shall be given you; seek, and ye shall find; knock, and it shall be opened unto you" (Luke 11:9).

When the last Bible study has been given and the last sermon preached, it will be through prayer—the asking—that we receive salvation, because Jesus comes into our hearts as an answer to prayer. Though the salvation Jesus has purchased on the cross for us is free, it is not ours unless we ask for it.

A baby is born completely helpless. Someone must provide for its every need. Yet if it is to survive, there are certain things that it must do for

"Ask, and it shall be given you; seek, and ye shall find; knock, and it shall be opened unto you."
—Luke 11:9.

itself. One of them is breathe.

Prayer is the breath of the soul. It's as natural for a newborn Christian to pray as it is for a newborn baby to breathe. When a Christian is born into the kingdom of God by grace through faith, one of the first acts of faith will be to pray. The apostle Paul met Jesus on the road to Damascus. Blinded by the vision of the Lord, he had to be led into the city, where he spent the next three days in prayer. When the Lord came to the prophet Ananias and told him to go visit Paul, Ananias was told, "Behold, he prayeth" (Acts 9:11).

A person born into the kingdom of heaven who doesn't pray will not survive for long. The prayers of others may sustain them temporarily, but sooner or later they must begin to pray on their own or their life in Christ will atrophy and disappear.

There are some things that others can do for us, but there are also things we must do for ourselves. We may hire someone to cook our food or be our personal physical trainer. Yet our health cannot be delegated to others. In the same way we can hire someone to teach us a particular subject, yet in the final analysis we must learn for ourselves. And so it is in the aspects of our lives that have to do with the eternal. No one else, no matter how saintly, can have a personal relationship with Jesus for another. Each must have a spiritual life that is uniquely their own.

A person who claims to have a relationship with God but who doesn't pray is not being honest, because prayer is communication with God. We can't have a relationship with someone with whom we do not communicate. It should therefore come as no surprise that in every generation men and women who have been people of God were without exception people of prayer.

During a prayer seminar I was conducting, a person came to me and said, "You claim that prayer changes the life. Well, Brother So-and-so prays all the time, and he's mean." Afterward I thought about what they had said. I suppose we would have to admit that praying doesn't necessarily mean that a person is a converted Christian. A person can pray and not be sincere. With everything there is the possibility of hypocrisy and deception. Just because a person says they pray doesn't prove that their heart is right with God. A person can do good works, give great sermons, and fill important positions in the church, and still be a Judas Iscariot.

Nevertheless, experience has shown that a person who spends time alone with God each day will seldom be guilty of being insincere in their relationship with the Lord. A true Christian will always feel their emptiness, weakness, and dependence on God; and for this reason they *must* pray. Because it is through prayer that we express our love for God, sorrow for our sins, and our longing for a holy life.

It could be said that true prayer is always the result of a broken heart. The heart that seeks the Lord with all its strength is the broken heart, and a continued broken heart is a condition for true prayer. It could not be clearer:

"The Lord is nigh unto them that are of a broken heart; and saveth such as be of a contrite spirit" (Psalm 34:18).

"The sacrifices of God are a broken spirit: a broken and a contrite heart, O God, thou wilt not despise" (Psalm 51:17).

"For thus saith the high and lofty One that inhabiteth eternity, whose name is Holy; I dwell in the high and holy place, with him also that is of a contrite and humble spirit, to revive the spirit of the humble, and to revive the heart of the contrite ones" (Isaiah 57:15).

"For all those things hath mine hand made, and all those things have been, saith the Lord: but to this man will I look, even to him that is poor and of a contrite spirit, and trembleth at my word" (Isaiah 66:2).

It is not natural for the carnal heart to pray. A person who is not born again may go through the motions of prayer, but it will be an act of the lips and not of the heart. The Scriptures leave no room for confusion when they say that the carnal heart is at enmity against God (Romans 8:7) and that spiritual things are spiritually discerned (1 Corinthians 2:14).

I was once talking with a person whose walk with the Lord had grown cold. I asked him if he ever prayed. He replied that he didn't, because he knew the changes that would come into his life if he did.

True prayer will break the hardest heart. Therefore, the greatest sin that we commit is the sin of prayerlessness. When we with all our heart truly seek Him, we will surely find Him, and the failures and defeats in the Christian life will be turned to success and victory because prayer and sinning don't go together in the same heart. Why? Because there is nothing that examines the heart more closely than the prayer of faith.

While prayer will consume sin, holding on to sin in the life will choke out prayer. The person I mentioned earlier who supposedly prayed all the time but was mean—he wasn't truly praying, because true prayer from the heart drives out meanness. Of course it must also be said that meanness not dealt with will sooner or later drive out prayer. The prophet made it clear when he wrote, "But your iniquities have separated between you and your God, and your sins have hid his face from you, that he will not hear" (Isaiah 59:2).

Betty and I did our first term of mission service in Pakistan. Our little freighter landed at the port city of Karachi, and then several days later we made a 900-mile trip north by air. We were assigned to what was then the Pakistan Union School, which was about 30 miles from the large city of Lahore.

When Betty and I first decided that we wanted to serve in the mission field, we asked few questions. Truth be told, we didn't know what questions to ask! We were willing to go wherever we were sent and to live wherever we were assigned.

We were pleasantly surprised to discover that the school was located in a rural environment. The water on the campus was cool and clean and came from deep wells, and we were able to have a garden nearly year round. In this country setting I decided I would raise chickens as the other missionaries did. They had white leghorns, which are proven egg layers. But I would go one better, I decided. I would raise more than just leghorns; I would make chickens my hobby. So before it was over, I had at least six or seven varieties, including beautiful Polish hens, which are black with a plume of white feathers growing out of the tops of their heads.

Unfortunately, we never got many eggs from these hens. The fancy varieties are not bred to be prolific layers. But one of the many things I learned about chickens is that chickens eat all day long. In fact, if they are not eating most of the time, something is wrong. One day I noticed that a Black Minorca hen wasn't eating. I suspected something was wrong, but for a day or so I didn't separate her from the rest of her flock. When she didn't show improvement, I decided I would put her in a separate pen. In the meantime, I went to the school library and began to read whatever I could find on the subject of diseases in chickens. One book I found had a chapter that seemed to describe exactly the symptoms I had observed. I concluded that the hen had what the book diagnosed as an impacted craw. But not to worry; there followed step-by-step instructions as to what to do about it, which was to perform surgery and clean out the craw.

There just happened to be a small clinic on the campus that hadn't been used for a number of years, and it included a little operating room. After reading more on the subject, I decided that the time had come to intervene surgically in the life of the chicken. So taking the book in one hand and clutching the chicken under my arm, I marched to the operating room.

I reasoned that one need not have completed a residency at the Mayo Clinic to be able to follow the simple directions. They were clear and humane. I carefully followed the instructions one step at a time. First, I plucked off the feathers over the area that was to be opened up. Then I sterilized the place where the incision was to be made and carefully made the incision. Through all of this the chicken did nothing to protest and was actually calm and quiet. On opening the craw, I discovered it was just as I had suspected—the craw was badly impacted. Closely following the directions, I cleaned out the area and sewed up first the craw and then the incision.

The instructions said that when the surgery was over, the bird should be put in a quiet place where it could rest and recover. I found such a place. First laying her on a towel, I then covered her with a basket so that it would be dark and quiet. I had to make a trip to Lahore and would be gone for several hours. I would check on her when I got back. Mission accomplished. Needless to say, I felt proud of myself.

When I returned from the city, I went to check on the patient and discovered that, although the operation had been a complete success, the chicken had died.

There are two things to learn from this story. One is obvious—don't ask me to operate on your sick chickens. The other is that it's true that when chickens lose their appetites, something is wrong with them.

Just as a healthy chicken has an appetite, so a person who is born again will have an appetite for the things of God and for all that is spiritual. Sometimes we describe a person who has recently become a Christian as having a "first love" experience. However, with the passage of time can also come a growing indifference and a lack of desire for spiritual things. This should not be something we accept as normal but should be cause for alarm, because it is an early sign of spiritual disease and eventual death.

A healthy Christian is *always* a praying Christian. A person who neglects prayer sooner or later will pay a price. To neglect prayer will result in an inevitable spiritual slide downward. It may be hardly noticeable at first, but eventually the symptoms will be unmistakable:

1. Heartfelt prayer soon becomes only empty words and a form.
2. The person's values become like those of the world.
3. They begin to talk less and less about God and about spiritual things.
4. Private time alone with God becomes less and less frequent, until at last it disappears altogether.
5. Resisting sin becomes less and less important, until it is resisted only when it would have the most serious consequences.

Prayerlessness has far-reaching consequences. If a church appears to be dead, it's because in that church prayer has died. Therefore, if there is to be revival, reformation, and renewal in the church, there must be a revival of prayer in the lives of its members.

It has been said that there are three kinds of churches. There is the church in which there is an opening prayer, a pastoral prayer, a prayer for the offering, and of course the benediction. Then there is the church that has a prayer ministries department. The third kind of church is a living church where everything that happens in every phase of church life is bathed in prayer.

On one occasion I preached in a church in which I noticed in the bulletin that after the worship service there would be a meeting of the prayer warriors. After standing at the door and shaking hands with the congregation, I returned to the front of the church to pray with the group. The group consisted of the pastor, a teenage boy, and three women.

As the little group knelt and prayed together, I wondered where the elders, the deacons, and the deaconesses were. I wondered where the Sabbath school superintendent was. Where were the Community Services leader and the Pathfinder leader?

I believe with all my heart that the time has come when those who are the leaders of the church should be men and women of prayer. How can I be a legitimate leader of the church if I am not spiritual? How can I be a spiritual leader if I am not a man of prayer?

I'm thankful we have those faithful persons in every church who have answered God's call to pray. I'm thankful for those whom we call prayer warriors. Yet we must not delegate the spiritual life of the church to the department of prayer ministries. If we are to be healthy physically, emotionally, or spiritually, we must not expect others to do for us what we must do for ourselves, and that is develop our own prayer life.

Contrary to popular belief, prayer is not something we are obliged to do when we can't do anything else. Prayer is something that we *must* do if we are to stay alive spiritually and grow in grace.

Prayer occupied a prominent place in the life of our Lord when He was here on this earth. In the early morning (Mark 1:35), late at night, and sometimes all night Jesus could be found in prayer. If Jesus was a man of prayer, how can a mortal man or woman who doesn't spend much time in prayer call himself or herself a follower of Jesus?

Prayer is a life-and-death matter because it is the means God has appointed for our receiving mercy and obtaining grace. "Let us therefore come boldly unto the throne of grace, that we may obtain mercy, and find grace to help in time of need" (Hebrews 4:16). It shouldn't come as a surprise that James would correctly diagnose the cause of our spiritual weakness when he wrote, "Ye have not because ye ask not" (James 4:2).

It can be safely said that our spiritual condition at any particular moment is a direct reflection of our prayer life. Before a baby is born, its mother's blood provides its oxygen. But at birth if it's going to survive, it must begin to breathe for itself. Prayer is the breath of the soul. Don't hold your breath!

Points to Consider
1. A good administrator will delegate authority, but a person who tries to delegate their spiritual life to someone else is bound to fail.
2. A person can be a religious leader without prayer, but a person who is a spiritual leader will always be a person of prayer.

Some Things to Pray About
1. That the Holy Spirit will convict me when I forget to pray.
2. That the Lord will make me a prayer model for my family and friends.

CHAPTER 2

WHEELIN' AND DEALIN' PRAYER

O ne of the first things that a person needs to learn when they enter certain cultures is the art of bargaining. While in the Western cultures most things have a "fixed price," in other parts of the world the price you pay depends on how good you are at bargaining.

When we landed in Pakistan, the expatriates introduced us to the fine art of bargaining. They told us that a merchant will often double the price of a particular item, and you aren't being rude when you counter by offering them only half their asking price.

Bargaining can make a person feel cheap, especially if the vendor is a poor person selling a souvenir, and here I am trying to get them to lower the price from $5 to $2.50. The little boy or girl who is selling is lucky to make a profit of 50 cents a day, and I'm trying to save myself a couple dollars. How mean and cheap can one be?

But not following certain protocol of bargaining could have complications beyond saving a dollar or two. I learned that if we didn't agree on

"If ye then, being evil, know how to give good gifts unto your children, how much more shall your Father which is in heaven give good things to them that ask Him?"
—Matthew 7:11.

a price before the time came to pay, the seller could protest loudly, a crowd could quickly gather, and things could become tense. For this reason, before I went shopping or rode in a taxi I would ask what the going rate was. When the merchants knew that I knew the true value of their offering, there would rarely be any argument.

In bargaining, a person tries to get as much as they can for as little an investment as possible. It's the old saw "I'll scratch your back if you scratch mine." There is no doubt that life is about give and take. If you want to get ahead, the prevailing practice is that you must take more than you give.

Every culture has its form of bargaining. In Western cultures business deals are negotiated. In a negotiation, both parties must be satisfied. This process is better than bargaining, because things are more likely to be out in the open. At its best, negotiation tries to be fair.

Sometimes a person tries to get what they want by overt or covert manipulation. Often when we want something we're afraid just to come right out and ask for it. So we hint, coax, charm, or even wheedle. Some consider these techniques to be skills. Admittedly, while they may get you what you want, they can easily cheapen a relationship. In a relationship in which one person is manipulating the other, respect will be lost.

Much of our life is about bargaining, negotiating, and otherwise making deals. Among huge retailing companies there is competition that seeks to offer the better deal. Sometimes I have wondered what life in heaven can possibly be like when so much of our existence here is about "wheelin' and dealin'" (I wonder what a person who is a born salesperson will do to exercise their talents in heaven!)

What does all this have to do with prayer? A lot. In our prayers we often try to make deals with God or otherwise negotiate an answer that is to our liking.

Is it wrong to try to cut a deal with God? Is our communication with God supposed to include bargaining, negotiating, coaxing, or even threatening?

WHEELIN' AND DEALIN' PRAYER

If you are like me, somewhere along the line in your prayer life you may have done all of the above. It could sound something like: "God, if You will do thus and so, I will do such and such." We may not like to admit we bargain, negotiate, or otherwise try to make deals in our prayers. But if we would only listen to ourselves once in a while, we might be surprised. The average person would have to admit that in their prayers they tend to make a lot of promises. But someone may ask, What is wrong with making promises to God?

There is a lot of Bible precedent for making promises to God. One that immediately comes to mind is the experience of Hannah. Her husband, Elkanah, had another wife with whom he had children. Hannah had none, and the other wife wouldn't let her forget it. One year it was really getting to her, and so Hannah went to the tabernacle and promised God that if He would give her a son, she would dedicate him to serve the Lord. The result was Samuel. The rest is history.

Someone else may ask, "But isn't the Sabbath school Investment program about making promises to God?"

So it is. You know how it goes. We pray, "Lord, I have an apple tree in my orchard that doesn't bear fruit anymore. If You make it bear fruit, I will give half the proceeds for Investment."

Aside from the fact that "promises are made to be broken" (I am surely glad God doesn't sue us for breach of contract), I have no objection to making promises to God. Experience has demonstrated that, as in the case of the mother of Samuel and in other important instances, God has often obliged when the prayer was based on a promise.

When we contemplate the role of making promises in prayer, the question that occurs is: Once we have established a relationship with our heavenly Father, must we feel that somehow in order to maintain it we must make promises—i.e., "Lord, I'll do this for You if You will do that for me"?

Think about it for a moment. In life's closest relationships we don't need to hint, coax, charm, wheedle, bargain, negotiate, or even make promises. The highest and best way to get something from someone, particularly someone we love and who we know loves us, is simply to ask.

Asking is one of the most intimate methods of communication, because it creates freedom for the one being asked. They are now free to accept, decline, add to, or take away from the request. Put another way, asking is a freedom-giving request.

Obviously, asking for a favor can be risky. It is risky because it gives the choice away. It lets go of control. Asking means allowing the other person to choose their response. A person who gets right to the point and just asks must be willing to accept either yes or no as an answer.

Some might believe that when the Bible says to ask, this too could be interpreted as wheelin' and dealin', bargaining, or negotiating. However, the conditions for answered prayer are not based on tit for tat or I'll scratch your back if you'll scratch mine. They are based on the relationship we have with God. Prayer is communicating with God, and, to be effective, communication must be based on a relationship.

Notice what word the following texts have in common:

Ephesians 3:20: "Now unto him that is able to do exceeding abundantly above all that we *ask* or think, according to the power that worketh in us."

James 1:6: "But let him *ask* in faith, nothing wavering. For he that wavereth is like a wave of the sea driven with the wind and tossed."

1 John 5:14: "And this is the confidence that we have in him, that, if we *ask* any thing according to his will, he heareth us."

When Scripture speaks of asking, it means choosing something or wanting something at a heartfelt level. It means craving something that we need very badly. The texts noted above and others establish that for our part when we come to God in prayer, He expects us simply to present before Him our heartfelt needs. In this sense, asking is not checking God out, testing the water, or otherwise the equivalent of buying a lottery ticket.

WHEELIN' AND DEALIN' PRAYER

For some, prayer is often what could be termed in computer language a "backup." Pray about it, but have Plan B ready. Neither should prayer be a last resort, as in "When all else fails, pray about it." This tendency may spring out of the nonexistent but oft-quoted text "God helps them that help themselves."

A close relative of mine developed cancer. A date for surgery was arranged. Two weeks before the surgery was to take place, our extended family came together for an anointing service. This service is usually requested when every other remedy has failed. To some it's seen as a type of last rites. We felt differently. As a family we decided that we should bring the problem to Jesus first rather than last.

Praying about something should not mean we now take no responsibility or initiative. Prayer is not something we do instead of doing something about the problems of life, but rather it should be what we do before we set out to try to solve a particular problem.

In our family prayer we simply turned the matter over to the Lord. We asked Him to be with us as a family through the ordeal that was about to come. We asked Him to guide the doctors and the nurses who would participate in the procedure.

By the way, have you noticed that many times when we ask the Lord to do something for us and the outcome is favorable, we tend to thank everyone who had a part except the One who made it all happen? We must remind ourselves that when we ask Jesus to do something for us and our prayer is answered, we ought to thank God before we thank the doctor or give credit to some wonder drug. But it seems that is the way it has always been. When Jesus healed the 10 lepers, only one came back to say thanks (Luke 17:17).

I often tell people that if they or someone they love gets sick, they probably don't want to call for me to pray for them. If you expect to see a show of force or power, you might be disappointed. You see, I don't make it complicated. I don't insist, I don't "storm the gates of heaven," I don't make promises. When I pray, I simply ask.

There are some who sincerely believe that if you pull out all the stops in prayer, God will most surely say yes. One woman assured me,

IF WITH ALL YOUR HEART

"I'm sure that if I agonized with the Lord, He would answer me."

I can understand how a person would be in agony over a particular situation in their life, but I am not sure that agonizing is the silver bullet that makes God respond favorably to our petition. God is nicer than we are, and we really don't need to twist His arm.

I like Matthew 7:11: "If ye then, being evil, know how to give good gifts unto your children, how much more shall your Father which is in heaven give good things to them that ask him?"

When I looked up the word "prayer" in the dictionary, I found that it is rooted in the Latin *precarius*. We use the word "precarious" when something is . . . well, when something is precarious, in the sense that something could go either way. Precarious means being dependent on circumstances beyond one's control; uncertain, unstable, insecure; dependent on the will or pleasure of another; or liable to be withdrawn or lost at the will of another.

As I contemplate the meaning of the word, I can understand better now the deeper meaning of prayer. Prayer is a precarious activity, because when rightly understood it gives the freedom of choice to another—that is, to God. In a real sense when we truly ask from our hearts, we are actually surrendering our will to God.

In its highest sense, asking is an act of faith. To have faith in God is to ask. Of course, asking is possible only with someone we love and trust, because we are in effect turning the choice over to the one who is being asked.

It's easy to understand why we get into the habit of bargaining, negotiating, manipulating, or trying to sign on the dotted line. In the workaday world it's a jungle out there, and the rule is the survival of the fittest. We feel we must be in control.

True prayer from the heart doesn't need to be complicated. If with all our hearts we seek Him, we know He hears us. We don't need to persuade the Beneficent One to be beneficent, and we don't need to feel that we have to try to persuade Him to give us what we really need.

When Jesus talked with Nicodemus that night long ago, He said that unless we become as little children we cannot see the kingdom of heaven. When little children have a need, they simply ask mommy and daddy for it.

I almost decided to title this chapter "When All Else Fails, Ask." If before you read this chapter you had been making deals with God, I hope that here at the end you can feel safe now to simply ask. In a very real sense, asking is the way we surrender our will to God. It's all right to ask.

But if prayer is about the will of God, and we have the promise in Philippians 4:19: "But my God shall supply all your need according to his riches in glory by Christ Jesus," then why do I even need to ask?

That will be the subject of the next chapter.

Points to Consider

1. Making a deal with God can tend to put our will ahead of His.
2. Don't wait to pray until all else fails; pray before you start.

Some Things to Pray About

1. That God will forgive us for making our relationship with Him conditional.
2. That He will forgive us for giving credit to the doctor or medicine before we give credit to Him.

CHAPTER 3

IF GOD ALREADY KNOWS, WHY PRAY?

"Your Father knoweth what things ye have need of, before ye ask him."

—Matthew 6:8.

In the last chapter we learned that the best relationships are based on simply asking, and that in asking we are surrendering control to the One being asked. If in the final analysis prayer is a process of surrendering our will to the will of God, and He already knows what we need, a person could come to the conclusion Why pray? *Que sera sera.*

Questions raised by unbelievers take the matter a step further and are based on the premise that absolute wisdom doesn't need to be informed of our desires, that absolute goodness doesn't need to be prompted to beneficence, or that an immutable and impassable God cannot be affected by humankind.

C. S. Lewis, in his book *The Seeing Eye and Other Selected Essays From Christian Reflections* (Ballandine Books, New York, 1967), has a chapter entitled "Petitionary Prayer: A Problem Without an Answer."

Lewis divides prayers of request into two categories. One he calls Pattern A, the other Pattern

B. He identifies Pattern A as the request based on the Model Prayer, "Thy will be done on earth as it is in heaven." He contends that this would seem to make all prayer conditional. This kind of prayer isn't a guarantee that God will give us what we request.

Lewis suggests that using the phrase "Thy will be done" in our prayers sounds as if God is saying, "You can ask for anything you want, but I will give you only what I want you to have."

It would be like a father who promises his son that he will give him whatever he wants for his birthday. The child asks for a bicycle; his father gives him a math book. Of course, in the long run the book will be more useful to the boy than the bike. But there is a problem. The father told the boy he would give him whatever he wanted. The problem in this case isn't with the book but with the promise.

The illustration seems to add fuel to the argument that if God already knows, why pray? Because no matter what one asks for, He will do as He pleases anyway.

Prayer Pattern B Lewis describes as the prayers throughout Scripture that seemed to have been answered, not through faith, but because of faith. We may be familiar with several examples that are found in the New Testament.

There is a story in Matthew 9:19-22: "And Jesus arose, and followed him, and so did his disciples. And, behold, a woman, which was diseased with an issue of blood twelve years, came behind him, and touched the hem of his garment: for she said within herself, If I may but touch his garment, I shall be whole. But Jesus turned him about, and when he saw her, he said, Daughter, be of good comfort; *thy faith* hath made thee whole. And the woman was made whole from that hour."

Jesus healed the centurion's servant with the words "As thou hast believed, so be it done unto thee" (Matthew 8:13). And there are other instances, such as the healing of the Canaanite woman's daughter (Matthew 15:28).

But the text that seems to be the trump card for the argument that faith is the secret of answered prayer is the one in Matthew 21:21: "Jesus answered and said unto them, Verily I say unto you, If ye have faith, and doubt not, ye shall not only do this which is done to the fig tree, but also if ye shall say unto this mountain, Be thou removed, and be thou cast into the sea; it shall be done."

In Pattern B nothing is said about asking for something that is the will of God. Faith seems to take on a life of its own—say the words, close your eyes really tight, and voilà, there you have it.

C. S. Lewis closes the chapter without resolving the apparent dichotomy. But we would-be petitioners can't. How we communicate with God (through Plan A, Plan B, or some other plan) reflects who we think He is and what He is like. Therefore, it's important that as we grow in grace we resolve as much as possible what may seem otherwise to be confusing concepts.

The text noted at the beginning of this chapter may hold the key to understanding what apparently Lewis was unable to resolve:

"Your Father knoweth what things ye have need of, before ye ask him" (Matthew 6:8).

The key words in this verse are not "what things ye have need of" but "your Father," of course referring to our heavenly Father.

Prayer then begins not with knowing what to ask for or how to ask for it. Rather, it must begin in knowing *whom* we are asking. Not understanding who God is can result in our asking for some off-the-wall things and then wondering why our prayers never seem to be answered.

In Matthew 7:11 Jesus asks a rhetorical question. Having reminded His listeners that though they were not perfect parents (He didn't mince words here), they knew how to give good gifts to their children. He then said, "How much more shall your Father which is in heaven give good things to them that ask him?"

The key words in this text are "good things." We parents and grandparents love to give gifts to our children. From where Betty and I are as grandparents, we would probably have to say that we get even greater joy in giving gifts to our grandchildren than we did in giving gifts to our children. This is probably because we give gifts to our grandchildren for a different reason.

When we are parents, there is an expectation of giving. Even beyond the expectation, there is an often not-so-subtle pressure of "Daddy, I *have* to have such and such." In today's culture parents may feel that not only must they give gifts that are up to their children's expectations, but if their children don't have the latest of a particular item, people in their own social circle may look down on them.

Not all the toys on the toy shelves could necessarily be classified as "good gifts." Not all gifts are necessarily good gifts. If we are to resolve what may appear to be a contradiction concerning prayer, we must learn what our heavenly Father considers to be "good gifts."

Though I remember buying caps, I can't remember ever having a cap pistol. My father didn't believe children should play as though they were shooting people. When I was 8 or 9 years old, I decided that I wanted a BB gun. A BB gun is not something one plays cops and robbers with. From my perspective, I planned to use it for target practice, or at least that was what I told Dad. I don't remember how long I had to ask for it, only that on some special occasion—it could have been my birthday—Dad finally bought me a single-shot BB gun.

I must have decided that the gun could be used for more than merely shooting cans or trying to break bottles. One day I noticed a neighborhood boy several years younger than I was playing outside with his dog. I happened to have my gun with me, and on the spur of the moment, when the dog was resting beside the boy, I decided to sting it with a BB.

Unfortunately I aimed down the barrel of the gun with the wrong eye, and when I pulled the trigger the shot hit the little boy in the face just below the eye. I can hardly bear to think of what could have happened.

Needless to say, my dad took the gun away from me and hid it. But one day when he wasn't around I discovered where it was, and then, from time to time when he was at the office, I would sneak it out and do some shooting. My luck didn't last very long. One day he found out what I was doing and broke the gun across his knee.

In this life our fathers gave us gifts. They may not have always been good gifts. Our heavenly Father, however, gives only good gifts. James 1:17 says: "Every good gift and every perfect gift is from above, and cometh down from the Father of lights, with whom is no variableness, neither shadow of turning." Things would go a lot differently for us in our prayer life, and, for that matter, in every aspect of our life, if we knew our heavenly Father better.

By the way, though my dad broke my gun, he didn't stop loving me or giving me food and shelter. I say this because the Scriptures tell us that there are some things our heavenly Father does for us without our having to ask, and He not only does these things for those who love Him but also for those who don't. "For he maketh his sun to rise on the evil and on the good, and sendeth rain on the just and on the unjust" (Matthew 5:45).

Not only does God cause the sun to shine on the just and the unjust, He is also the one responsible for keeping our hearts beating 2.5 billion times in a lifetime, pumping 250,000 gallons of blood through 100,000 miles of blood vessels. He is the one who makes a carrot out of a carrot seed and then in digestion processes it into compounds to sustain our lives. For these kinds of things we don't need to ask, but we should give thanks!

So having been assured that as our Father God is interested in giving us only good gifts, we should try to steer our prayers from that which we *think* is good for us, which in fact may or may not be good, to that which is in fact good for us. Without always knowing the exact details, we can discover this through a study of the Word of God.

The bottom line is that God doesn't ask us to tell Him something that He already knows. But He asks us to pray so that we may be capable of receiving what He is preparing to give.

At this stage of their lives, several of our grandsons are into Legos. This is OK for now, but hardly for when they are ready to go to college. As we grow and develop in our spiritual lives, we may expect that our perspectives will mature and become increasingly like those of our heavenly Father's until His desire for us becomes our desire for ourselves.

But what about the texts that say that all you have to do is have faith and God will do it your way? We have seen that, as our heart is more and more united with the heart of God, we may indeed ask what we want. But more and more, what we want will be what He wants for us and then, of course, it will be done.

Our prayers will be answered not because we have faith in faith, but because we have faith in God. The apparent contradiction that C. S. Lewis couldn't resolve is no problem at all when we read the texts this way. To the woman who touched His garment, the Lord said, "Daughter, be of good comfort; thy faith *[in Me]* hath made thee whole" (Matthew 9:22). And to the centurion: "As thou hast believed *[in Me],* so be it done unto thee" (Matthew 8:13).

And the text about moving mountains is really saying, "Don't worry. If you have faith in God, and don't doubt, there's nothing God can't do for you that is for your eternal good. Even if it means having to move mountains, He will do it."

Points to Consider

1. At times the Bible may seem to present certain contradictions, but when rightly understood, they are not.
2. The time must come when what we want is what God wants for us.

Some Things to Pray About

1. That God will show us from applications of His Word what is really good for us.
2. That we be prepared to receive what He is willing to give us.

TELLING IT LIKE IT IS

"In the day when I cried thou answeredst me, and strengthenedst me with strength in my soul."

—Psalm 138:3.

F or 12 years I worked with ADRA (Adventist Development and Relief Agency). ADRA works closely with local governments to relieve the suffering of their most vulnerable populations and to develop long-range programs that will improve their health and overall well-being. During those years I had the opportunity of traveling to many countries of the world.

I've seen some of the most pathetic situations that this world has to offer—grinding poverty, squalid refugee camps, pitiful lepers, malnourished children whose mouths and eyelids were covered with flies.

Also in the course of my work it was necessary to interact with governmental leaders and decision-makers. I've been in the company of presidents of countries and of cabinet-level ministers.

Working in high government-to-government circles, there are certain protocols. A protocol is a set ceremony or formality to be followed in a particular situation. There are things you say and don't say and other things that must be said only in certain ways.

On several occasions I testified before committees of the United States House of Representatives on behalf of the work being done by international volunteer agencies. It was an interesting and educational experience.

At important events it is rare that a person who is testifying will speak extemporaneously. They are more likely to read from a prepared statement. I was interested to discover that the person is actually permitted to edit their own testimony even after it has been presented to the members of the committee but before it becomes part of the permanent record.

What does this have to do with prayer? There are some who, for some reason or another, have come to believe that when we pray we must use a certain protocol. Not only a certain protocol, but also a certain language and even a certain tone of voice. It is not uncommon for some to speak to God in what might be termed a form of religious diplomatic language.

Not only might their language change when they pray, but also their whole demeanor. Whereas one moment they are open and relaxed, in prayer they become somewhat formal, even nervous and guarded in what they say and the way they say it.

While protocol and diplomacy are important in relationships between nations, forced political correctness in prayer can result in frustrating its purpose and make it largely ineffective—at least as far as the one who is praying is concerned.

Some of the most beautiful prayers ever spoken were presented under the inspiration of the Holy Spirit. Later written down and even set to music, these are the psalms of David. The psalms of David are from the heart. Though David was educated from an early age in the protocols of a royal court and one day became a king himself, he never confused his relationships in the court with his relationship to God.

In negotiating with Hiram, the king of Tyre, to prepare materials to build the Temple, David must have been diplomatic in every sense of the word. But when he was talking with God, he was direct and to the point. Reading the prayers of David, one doesn't have to call in the legal department to understand what he meant to say. David was a poet and his prayers reflect his gift, yet in the poetry is heard the feelings of his heart.

As I read the prayers of David, two things impress me: (1) he expressed his heartfelt feelings, whatever they might have been at the time, and (2) though at times he was bitter and angry with his enemies, he didn't see God as his problem but as the answer to his problem. He knew who his enemy was, and he knew it wasn't God.

At times he would express his frustration and impatience, such as when he prayed, "Why standest thou afar off, O Lord? why hidest thou thyself in times of trouble?" (Psalm 10:1).

When almost in desperation he prayed, "My God, my God, why hast thou forsaken me? why art thou so far from helping me?" (Psalm 22:1). And again: "How long wilt thou forget me, O Lord? for ever? how long wilt thou hide thy face from me? how long shall I take counsel in my soul, having sorrow in my heart daily? how long shall mine enemy be exalted over me? Consider and hear me, O Lord my God: lighten mine eyes, lest I sleep the sleep of death" (Psalm 13:1-3).

At other times, even though surrounded by difficulties, he seemed more rational and prayed, "Lord, how are they increased that trouble me! many are they that rise up against me. Many there be which say of my soul, There is no help for him in God. Selah. But thou, O Lord, art a shield for me; my glory, and the lifter up of mine head" (Psalm 3:1-3).

When you speak to God from the heart, it's not necessary for your prayer to be organized, clearly stated, or even consistent. We can freely reveal to Him our inmost needs and desires. We can share our deepest thoughts, even when they are intolerable or unthinkable.

When we pray, it would be well for us to begin our prayers with thanks and praise to God. Though it is perfectly permissible as far as God is concerned to get right to the point and spit out our pent-up emotions, it is not always the best for us. When we begin our prayers with thanks and praise, it doesn't avoid or hide what we really feel but actually initiates the healing process we so badly need.

I had a friend in college who also studied for the ministry. Little did Betty and I know that a few years later we would meet him and his wife in Pakistan. They were arriving for mission service as we were leaving.

Not many years later I heard that the wife had died suddenly. Sitting in my office, my friend recounted how at 5:00 in the morning as they were in bed his wife suddenly moved in a way that startled him. He reached his hand over and, touching her, asked, "Honey, are you all right?"

She never answered. At 37 years of age she was dead.

With tears in his eyes he recounted how his whole world had suddenly caved in. He went into what might be called a spiritual and emotional free fall. When friends suggested that he pray, he discovered he couldn't. They urged him to read the Bible, but he didn't want to. When someone would speak of the coming of Jesus and the resurrection, he couldn't believe it. A black curtain had fallen across his life. To him it was an impenetrable darkness.

One day he received a letter from a person he didn't even know. It said, "I know what you are going through. It is in the memories. Look back."

Normally we say that a person should not look back but only go forward. But perhaps not in such a case as this. You see, my friend had lost all his connections. To be able to go forward into the unknown he had to go back into memory. He had to return in his mind to that which even death could not take away, and that was his memories of her.

There may come a time in your life when the pain and grief are so great that you lose the desire to pray. It is possible that your heart could be so broken that your prayers, in the short term at least, don't seem to bring relief. Beginning your prayers by remembering and recounting the ways God has been with you in the past can often alleviate this feeling.

IF WITH ALL YOUR HEART

Lately I have been trying to intentionally begin my prayers by connecting the often painful challenges of the present with the many times the Lord has heard my prayers and has been with me in the past. The promise is that there is no trial so big but that He will make it possible for us to get through it.

"There hath no temptation taken you but such as is common to man: but God is faithful, who will not suffer you to be tempted above that ye are able; but will with the temptation also make a way to escape, that ye may be able to bear it" (1 Corinthians 10:13). Reminding ourselves of this promise will sustain us when it appears as though there is no hope.

David had his ups in downs, and his prayers reflect this fact. On one occasion he was so upset he prayed that God would destroy not only his enemies but also their wives and children. He prayed that God would wipe out even their memory from the earth. But when he got to the end of his litany of bitterness, he told God what the real problem was when he said, "But do thou for me, O God the Lord, for thy name's sake: because thy mercy is good, deliver thou me. For I am poor and needy, and my heart is wounded within me" (Psalm 109:21, 22).

In these verses David is saying, "Lord, have mercy on me, because I really need You." The real struggle was not with his enemies but with his own heart, and he knew that only God could heal his wounded spirit.

The apostle Peter tells us that we should cast all our cares upon Him (1 Peter 5:7). Psalm 55:22 urges us to cast our burden on the Lord and promises that if we do, He will sustain us.

Our prayers don't need to follow diplomatic protocol. We should not hesitate to express our deepest feelings. God Himself invites us to tell it like it is. "Produce your cause, saith the Lord; bring forth your strong reasons, saith the King of Jacob" (Isaiah 41:21).

On one occasion Jeremiah took God at His word. In a moment of near despair he prayed, "O Lord, thou hast deceived me, and I was deceived: thou art stronger than I, and hast prevailed" (Jeremiah 20:7).

The point is that when we pray we can tell God exactly how we feel. We may be angry, bitter, or discouraged, but He isn't. He is the same yesterday, today, and forever (Hebrews 13:8).

When I was a child it was not uncommon for farmers to use horses in plowing and cultivating their fields. One day I was watching a young man working with his white horse. My neighbor said, "See that young man? He has a nervous condition. Sometimes when he has an attack he will pick up a board and beat the horse."

I was horrified. I asked my neighbor what the horse did when the young man beat on him.

My neighbor replied, "The horse seems to know that something is wrong with his master, so he just stands there and takes it."

Our God is gracious, long-suffering, and merciful (Exodus 34:6). Even when we're experiencing a fit of anger, we can feel free to tell Him how we feel. He'll just listen. He just takes it. He won't chide us or put us down. For those who seek Him with all their heart, He will have mercy and will abundantly pardon (Isaiah 55:7).

I've found that sometimes when my feelings get bottled up and I don't know exactly what I want to say, reading from the Psalms can actually help me express myself. Who can say it better than David when he cried, "I will extol thee, O Lord; for thou hast lifted me up, and hast not made my foes to rejoice over me. O Lord my God, I cried unto thee, and thou hast healed me. O Lord, thou hast brought up my soul from the grave: thou hast kept me alive, that I should not go down to the pit. Sing unto the Lord, O ye saints of his, and give thanks at the remembrance of his holiness. For his anger endureth but a moment; in his favour is life: weeping may endure for a night, but joy cometh in the morning" (Psalm 30:1-5).

Thank You, Lord; I couldn't have said it better myself.

Points to Consider
1. Don't try to keep any secrets from God.
2. We need not fear for the future unless we forget the way that the Lord has led us in the past.

IF WITH ALL YOUR HEART

Some Things to Pray About

1. That we will remember that the only solution for the grief of this world is the coming of Jesus and the resurrection.
2. That when we suffer we will get closer to Jesus and not be driven away by discouragement.

CHAPTER 5

I'D RATHER
NOT, BUT . . .

I t is well to recognize that there will always be a tension and even sometimes a contradiction between our desires and God's will. God Himself tells us that the root of the problem is that "my thoughts are not your thoughts, neither are your ways my ways. . . . For as the heavens are higher than the earth, so are my ways higher than your ways, and my thoughts than your thoughts" (Isaiah 55:8, 9).

We could phrase it another way by saying that we're not on God's wavelength, or that we don't know where He is coming from. But God's nature is not the problem; we are. Of human nature it is written, "The heart is deceitful above all things, and desperately wicked: who can know it?" (Jeremiah 17:9).

Were it not for the fact that Jesus stands at the door of our hearts and knocks (Revelation 3:20); were it not for the fact that He has sent us the Holy Spirit to convict us of sin, of righteousness, and of judgment (John 16:13); were it not for the fact that the Word was made flesh and dwelt

"For I reckon that the sufferings of this present time are not worthy to be compared with the glory which shall be revealed in us."—Romans 8:18.

among us (John 1:14), the wall between us and our Maker could not be breached. Thank God, through Jesus Christ the wall has not only been breached, but has been taken away. Now communication—ongoing communication—between a holy God and a redeemed people is possible through His Word and the process of prayer.

My study of prayer always brings me back to the same place: The purpose of prayer is that the will of God will be discovered and implemented into our lives—and that it will be recognized and accepted in other's lives (this is called intercession).

I was once talking with someone about the will of God and expressing my conviction that the purpose for our existence is for His pleasure. The person seemed to have some problem with this, because they asked, "If we are to live only for His pleasure, what about us? Isn't that selfish?"

My answer was "Hardly." Inasmuch as we were made by Him, we can be complete only when we abide in Him (John 15:4, 5). There is never, under any circumstances, anything to be lost when we choose to do His pleasure. But sin, by its very nature, is at odds with the will of God. By instinct we want to be respectable sinners, whereas God wants us to be self-sacrificing saints.

In light of what you've just read, you may say, "Pastor O'Ffill, not to worry; I accept the will of God for my life."

There can be no doubt that this is a step in the right direction. You have decided to submit to the will of God. Yet is submission to the will of God the gold standard of the Christian life?

Merely to submit is to surrender, to succumb, to capitulate, or to yield. It is to bow or to defer. To submit, then, to the will of God doesn't necessarily mean that we are in agreement. While submission is not rebellion, neither is it necessarily acceptance. Although God accepts our surrender to His will, He wishes that we would go a step further and not only submit to His will, but be in conformity to it. While submitting to the will of God is passive, conformity to His will is active. There is an old saying that a person persuaded against their will is of the same opinion still. A person could conceivably be submitting to the will of God and not be in agreement with what God is trying to do in their life. To be conformed to the will of God means that we are willingly carrying out His wishes.

Although the Christian life begins with submission to the will of God, we must press on to the point where we can say, "I delight to do thy will, O my God" (Psalm 40:8).

There may be times, especially when things are dark or when we don't understand all that is going on, when we must fall back and stand only on our submission to God. Jesus Himself came to this point when He was in the Garden of Gethsemane. Suddenly it was as though the plug that since eternity had connected Him with His Father was being pulled. In agony and desperation He prayed, "O my Father, if it be possible, let this cup pass from me: nevertheless not as I will, but as thou wilt" (Matthew 26:39).

His prayer was one of submission. His request was "Father, if it is possible, let's not go through with this." But then He added the word "nevertheless." His prayer then was "Father, I don't want to go through with this. But be that as it may, I will do whatever You wish."

I'm sure that in your life as well as mine there are many times when we have prayed in effect, "O Lord, get me out of this." At times the trials and sufferings of this life become more than we can bear.

There are some who suggest that the reason we suffer is a lack of faith on our part. I have learned in my life that faith is not something that makes my problems or suffering of the moment go away; rather, it is faith in God that gets me through them.

When Jesus prayed, "If it be possible, let this cup pass from me," God's answer was to give Him strength to bear it. Some of the most profound thoughts concerning Christ in this respect are found in Hebrews 5:7-9: "Who in the days of his flesh, when he had offered up prayers and supplications with strong crying and tears unto him that was able to save him from death, and was heard in that he feared; though he were a Son, yet learned he obedience by the things which he suffered; and being made perfect, he became the author of eternal salvation unto all them that obey him."

IF WITH ALL YOUR HEART

In the book *Transforming Prayer* I describe what I term the false prayer and the true prayer. I explain that the false prayer is the one in which we seek to exploit the power of God and impose our will on Him. In the true prayer we seek to discover the will of God and to glorify His name. The prayer of faith, then, is not the one in which we try to convince God to do our wishes. Rather it is the prayer in which even in darkness and despair we determine to be faithful to Him and to His will.

Some years ago my wife and I were passing through very difficult trials in relationships with some of our children and grandchildren. A little family was breaking up, and we were nearly beside ourselves with grief and concern. Of course we were praying with all our hearts, yet it seemed that at least for the time being things were going from bad to worse.

One day in all sincerity Betty asked, "What good does it do to pray?"

She wasn't trying to be facetious. We were praying with all our hearts, but the problem seemed to be getting more complicated with every day.

We were asking for what we believed was the will of God for this particular situation, yet the problem was not going away. And so we found ourselves saying, "Lord, take this cup from us, but nevertheless, not our will but Thine be done."

While submission must be the baseline of our prayers, if we would grow in grace we must go on from submission to His will to conformity to His will. We must go on from mere acquiescence to agreement. It is at this point in the prayer life where the rubber meets the road.

It was a spirit of agreement that caused biblical giants of faith to be able to say, "My brethren, count it all joy when ye fall into divers temptations; knowing this, that the trying of your faith worketh patience. But let patience have her perfect work, that ye may be perfect and entire, wanting nothing" (James 1:2-4).

And: "In every thing give thanks: for this is the will of God in

Christ Jesus concerning you" (1 Thessalonians 5:18).

After recounting some of the hair-raising experiences through which he had passed in his travels, Paul continued, "In weariness and painfulness, in watchings often, in hunger and thirst, in fastings often, in cold and nakedness. Beside those things that are without, that which cometh upon me daily, the care of all the churches. Who is weak, and I am not weak? who is offended, and I burn not? If I must needs glory, I will glory of the things which concern mine infirmities" (2 Corinthians 11:27-30).

Though Scripture teaches that we should live one day at a time (Matthew 6:34), there are moments when, if we thought that today were all there was, we would throw up our hands in despair.

Once while speaking at a camp meeting in New England, I visited a graveyard that dated from the 1600s. I was deeply moved as I walked from gravestone to gravestone. It was impressive to notice that although there were a few who had died at a ripe old age, the majority had died young. Many had been laid to rest in their 30s, 40s, and 50s. Also there were a number of young children buried there. One inscription on a 12-year-old child's grave told that he had died while swimming in the river. I could only imagine his parents' grief.

This life is about suffering and finally about death. And if that were all, life would be nothing short of a mockery. But as we open our hearts to God in prayer, we can look from a present that, as in the case of Jesus in the garden, appears bleak and seemingly the end of the road, to something wonderful beyond. As I walked through the quiet graveyard, my mind was carried to a future in which those in the graves will hear His voice. It is this knowledge that gives us the hope to say with the apostle Paul, "For I reckon that the sufferings of this present time are not worthy to be compared with the glory which shall be revealed in us" (Romans 8:18).

We can move on from submission to His will to complete agreement with Him, because He is faithful that promised (Hebrews 10:23).

IF WITH ALL YOUR HEART

It is unfortunate that when we refer to the will of God it is usually in reference to some calamity. We must grow in our prayers until we see the will of God not as defeat but as victory. I heard of a woman who was actually pleased when God didn't answer her prayers the way she wanted, because then she knew that God's will was being done and not hers!

I don't think I would want to carry things that far. But I do want to get beyond resignation to rejoicing.

The story is told of a Scottish woman who earned a modest living peddling her wares along the roads of her country. When she came to an intersection, she would toss a stick into the air to determine which way to go.

On one occasion she was seen tossing the stick into the air not once but three times. When asked why, she replied, "Because the first two times it pointed a way I didn't want to go!"

Many of our prayers are like that. We ask God for guidance, but when He occasionally directs us down a dull or difficult road, we're not satisfied and prefer our own path.

There are two stories in Scripture that can be a help to us in this regard. One is when the disciples had fished all night and hadn't caught anything. In the morning Jesus came along and called out to ask them how it went. Peter shouted back that they hadn't caught anything. Jesus replied to him from the shore, "Throw your nets on the other side."

Right, Peter must have thought. *He must not have heard what I said.*

Though in disagreement and mumbling something about having already tried that, Peter went along. The story had a happy ending. But think how much better it would have been if Peter had been conformed to the will of Jesus and had said to the others with him, "Hey, boys, our troubles are over. Jesus is going to get us some fish."

Jesus' mother had it right at the wedding of Cana. A problem arose, and she went immediately to the One who could solve it. If she had been really sensitive, she might have been hurt by what Jesus said to her and might have replied, "Oh, never mind." But she didn't. She went to the servants and simply said, "Do whatever He tells you."

Our perspective on life will improve and the burdens we must bear will seem lighter when we move beyond "O Lord, do I have to?" to "I delight to do Thy will, O my God."

His ways are not our ways—His ways are better.

I asked for strength that I might achieve,
    I was made weak that I might obey.
I asked for health that I might do great things,
    I was given infirmity that I might be happy.
I asked for riches that I might be happy,
    I was given poverty that I might be wise.
I asked for power that I might have the praise of men,
    I was given weakness that I might feel the need of God.
I asked for all things that I might enjoy life,
    I was given life that I might enjoy all things.
I received nothing that I asked for, all that I hoped for,
    My prayer is answered.
        —R. H. Fitzhugh, "The Prayer of Paradox"

Points to Consider

1. It is better to submit than to resist.
2. It is better to be in conformity to the will of God than merely to submit to it.

Some Things to Pray About

1. That God will forgive us for resisting His will in our lives.
2. That He will give us a long-range view instead of a short-range view of what is important in our lives.

CHAPTER 6

WHEN NO
IS REALLY YES

"The sufferings of this present time are not worthy to be compared with the glory which shall be revealed in us."
—Romans 8:18.

S he was an attractive teenage blond. She lived with her family in Baltimore, Maryland. She loved to ride horses. It was July 30, 1967, and the family was spending a day at the Chesapeake Bay. Joni Eareckson decided to take a swim. She jumped headfirst off a dock, hitting her head hard at the bottom of the bay. Suddenly she couldn't feel her feet anymore. In fact, she couldn't feel anything. From that moment on, her life would never be the same.

Not only would Joni's life never be the same, but because God answered her prayer in a way she could never have imagined, the lives of countless others would be impacted for eternity.

What do you mean, God answered her prayer? Don't tell me she prayed that she would spend the rest of her life paralyzed.

Not at all; in fact she, her family, and friends prayed for a miracle. They prayed that somehow she would be healed. The answer at the time seemed to be no; but now looking back, they've discovered it was really yes.

WHEN NO IS REALLY YES

It is curious the manner in which we bring our most urgent requests to God. We often approach Him in ways we would never consider approaching our family doctor, or for that matter our auto mechanic.

When I go to the doctor, I tell him my symptoms the best I can, but I leave it to him to tell me what my problem is and what I ought to do about it. With the auto mechanic it is more complicated, because if the car doesn't happen to be malfunctioning when I drive it into his shop, he will tell me to bring it back when it is!

But when it comes to the problems of life, we poor mortals have a tendency to want to self-diagnose and prescribe our own remedy. We try to handle it ourselves, and only if it doesn't work will we take it to God in prayer.

Then we have the nerve to try to convince God that our solution is just what should be done and that He should do as we ask. In the end, when the expected result doesn't come about, we often conclude it was probably because we didn't have enough faith.

But could it be that our self-diagnosis was incorrect in the first place? And if not, maybe what we were prescribing was not in our best interest? This shouldn't surprise us, because Romans 8:26 tells us that we don't know how to pray as we ought. Often while it may seem that God has rejected our prayers, it may be that He has rejected only the way we insisted they be answered.

There are many instances in which God has apparently said no to the requests of godly men and women. Yet we discover in retrospect that the answer was actually not no but yes—perhaps no to the smaller prayer but yes to the true desires of the heart.

One of the most obvious examples in Scripture was the prayer of Moses to enter the Promised Land. For 40 years this man of God had one desire of his heart, and that was to lead his people into Canaan. One day he became upset and publicly disobeyed God. In spite of his prayers to be forgiven and to be able to enter into the Promised Land, he was laid to rest on a lonely mountaintop.

But it was not for long. God had an answer to Moses' prayer

that went beyond his wildest dreams. God permitted him to enter the Promised Land after all—the heavenly Canaan; and not only that, he was present one day to encourage Jesus in the most wonderful manifestation of the glory of God on the mountain we call the Mount of Transfiguration.

Later another giant of the faith, the apostle Paul, would pray for healing. We're not sure what his problem was. It may have been eye trouble. The apparent answer was no, but time would reveal that the prayer of Paul's heart would be answered.

"And lest I should be exalted above measure through the abundance of the revelations, there was given to me a thorn in the flesh, the messenger of Satan to buffet me, lest I should be exalted above measure. For this thing I besought the Lord thrice, that it might depart from me. And he said unto me, My grace is sufficient for thee: for my strength is made perfect in weakness. Most gladly therefore will I rather glory in my infirmities, that the power of Christ may rest upon me" (2 Corinthians 12:7-9).

It's rare that great men and women of God have not known sorrow.

Seventeen hundred years after Paul's time Adoniram Judson, the great missionary to Burma, prayed that the Lord would send him to save the lost. In his heart he longed to be able to minister to the heartaches and heartbreaks of others. His prayer to minister effectively to others was answered yes, but his prayer that his wife's life would be spared, and that his children would be healed was answered no. His prayer to be spared from spending time in prison was answered no so that his desire to be able to minister to those who were captives to sin would be answered yes. God gave Judson an answer to the prayer behind his prayers.

At significant times in my own life God has said no to my smaller prayer so that He could later say yes to my larger need.

When I accepted the call to be the ADRA director for the Chile Union Mission, my father lamented that it was too bad I had decided to leave the ministry to pass out old clothes.

It would later become apparent that although I may not have been in the pastoral ministry, I was surely doing more than passing out old clothes. Before many years had passed, our Chilean team initiated a feeding and medical program for the malnourished children of the country that was so successful it was adopted by the Chilean Ministry of Health.

As a result of this program and the success of an agricultural program in the country of Chad, ADRA began a move toward becoming an agency that would later work around the world in programs not only of disaster relief but of mother-child health, potable water and sanitation, and community development, to name just a few.

During the developmental stages of this department, I was in the middle of it all. Having been trained at Columbia Union College and the theological seminary at Andrews University, I now began to learn the craft of international development, which would include attending classes at the Massachusetts Institute of Technology. I have certificates from a number of classes sponsored by the Agency for International Development. I had the opportunity to testify before Congress, all the while traveling the world and meeting with presidents of nations and other government officials. It was an exciting, heady experience.

But circumstances arose and forces began to gather against me. Through it all, I prayed. It seemed from my point of view that the problems could be easily solved if the Lord chose to do so. Time went on, but circumstances did not improve. Eventually there was a reorganization, and I was reassigned to other responsibilities within the agency. I couldn't understand how this would happen. Why hadn't the Lord answered my prayer?

I became demoralized and decided to look for another job. A position became available in Florida, where my wife had been raised. All evidence indicated that this was the right move to make. However, moving to Florida wasn't the end of my sorrows but the beginning of new ones. Before long we began to have serious problems with one of our children.

IF WITH ALL YOUR HEART

It was at this period of my life that I turned desperately to the Lord. Although I had thought my future lay in international relief and development, I now found myself praying and preaching my heart out. The one who had for 12 years taught that there was religion in a loaf of bread and had begun to think bread was religion, was now learning that we do not live by bread alone.

True, as a young minister I dedicated myself to serve the Lord, and I have endeavored to do this throughout my ministry. Now at this point in my service I have come to the realization that my years in international development, though exciting, were not the pinnacle of my career. God had greater things for me. His no to my pleas to solve the problems in one area of my career was a yes to bring me back to a preaching ministry that has been the most fulfilling of my life. Although God has sometimes said no to the letter of my prayers, it is clear that the spirit of my prayers has been answered.

When they were young, sometimes my children would come to me and say, "Dad, I know you're going to say no, but . . . ," and then they would make their request. Sometimes I would surprise them and say yes, but more often than not their foregone conclusion was correct and I would say no.

Believe it or not, sometimes I noticed that the children were relieved. By saying no, I was confirming their own evaluation of the situation. The children seemed to know before they made the request that it was unwise, but they felt they must ask anyway. There was a conflict between what they wanted and what they knew was best for them.

If we as parents were to say yes to every whim that comes to the minds of our children, we would be doing them a disservice. To indulge their every request, especially when they suspect beforehand that it is probably not best, could frustrate the development of the perseverance and maturity they will need in later years.

God answers prayer in different ways. Sometimes He simply says yes. When He does, our faith immediately grows stronger and we feel better. Other times He says yes but there may be a long delay and/or the answer may come in a way that we didn't expect.

There are times He seems to say no, but looking back, we can see that it was really yes.

We must not try to box God in by our prayers that are often for an immediate need and that do not take into account the long view.

Once when I was giving a seminar at a camp meeting, I took particular notice of a husband and wife in the audience. As I preached, the man seemed to be drinking in what I was saying. It appeared he had a continual smile on his face. A day or so later the wife explained to me that her husband had recently been baptized, but not before she had prayed for him for 52 years!

For 52 years it seemed that God was not answering her prayers. What appeared to be a no was really a yes, but it would take years of patient praying to see the answer. Along the way she might have given up. The marriage might have broken up. But she continued to pray. The prayer of her heart was answered, albeit not in the time frame that she expected.

There is a beautiful benediction in Ephesians 3:20, 21: "Now unto him that is able to do exceeding abundantly above all that we ask or think, according to the power that worketh in us, unto him be glory in the church by Christ Jesus throughout all ages, world without end, Amen."

God wants to do for us even more than we ask. If we will, we can look back and see that God gives us even more than we bargained for. God's greater interest is the prayer behind our prayer. We must not limit Him as to how or when He will answer. We should not confine Him to only one way.

Someone may object and ask, "But what about the text that says, 'Delight thyself also in the Lord; and he shall give thee the desires of thine heart'" (Psalm 37:4)?

This text is interpreted by some to mean that if we assure the Lord that He is our delight, He will give us what we want, when we want it. But this is not what the text is saying. Think about it for a moment. If our delight is in the Lord and we make Him the object of our affection, it would only follow that the desire of our heart will be Him and that we will seek His will as the way for our lives.

Sometimes a delayed or disguised response is His way of giving us what we have been asking for all along. Before her accident, Joni had prayed that the Lord would change her and turn her life around. Although the accident was not part of His plan for her life, what He did in spite of the accident definitely was.

Points to Consider

1. Before you suspect that God has not answered your prayer, check to see whether in His kindness He has not actually given you more than you asked for.
2. We should not insist that God answer us in only one particular way. His ways are past finding out.

Some Things to Pray About

1. That He will give us the grace to be thankful to Him for everything, knowing that all things work together for good to them that love Him.
2. That God will forgive us for being upset when He says no.

CHAPTER 7

AN OUNCE OF PREVENTION

"Watch and pray, that ye enter not into temptation: the spirit indeed is willing, but the flesh is weak."
—Matthew 26:41.

Grandma used to say, "An ounce of prevention is worth a pound of cure." Her great-granddaughter would convert that to "28.3495 grams of prevention is worth 0.453592 kilograms of cure." But that just doesn't sound the same. Grandma had other sayings: "A stitch in time saves nine," and the one almost everyone understands: "Better safe than sorry."

In the material aspects of our lives, we understand what it means to take precautions. But somehow in the area of how the Christian life should be, many don't seem to have grasped the concept.

I value my house because it's the single largest investment I'll ever make. Therefore, there are fuses in the electrical system that will break the circuit if there's a short somewhere. We also have a termite bond on our house. An inspector comes out once a quarter to check the bait traps that have been placed around the perimeter of the building (we learned the hard way on that one, after the damage was done!).

I'm not alone in taking precautions. After

having been robbed two times, the bank on the corner where I do business installed a two-inch bulletproof barrier between the tellers and the customers. Every now and then a police car is parked in front of the bank. Even though there may be no officer on the premises, the cruiser serves as a scarecrow for any would-be robbers.

Military aircraft have high-tech equipment on board that senses when the plane is being "painted" by a beam of radar that serves as a guide path for missiles. When the alarm goes off, the pilot must immediately take evasive action. To ignore the warning would be to invite disaster.

The Christian life is dangerous. From that long-ago, nontechnical age the Bible writer calls on us to be on guard. "Be sober, be vigilant; because your adversary the devil, as a roaring lion, walketh about, seeking whom he may devour" (1 Peter 5:8).

That illustration doesn't mean much to most of us urbanites, but it would have meant a lot to the population of northern India. In the early part of the last century in the Nainital district the population was terrorized by a leopard that killed hundreds of people before it was shot by a professional hunter. For us in the twenty-first century, to speak of deadly animals may seem long ago and far away; but unfortunately we *do* understand the word "terrorist." If the apostle Peter were writing today, he might have said, "Don't let your guard down, because your enemy the devil, as a terrorist . . ."

In Jesus Christ the plan of salvation has all that is needed to clean up the debris in our lives resulting from the terror attack that sin wreaks on us. No matter the damage we have suffered, the promise is that "he is able also to save them to the uttermost that come unto God by him, seeing he ever liveth to make intercession for them" (Hebrews 7:25).

While we rejoice to claim this promise, there are unfortunately many who have not yet caught the vision of the promises in Romans 6:14, "For sin shall not have dominion over you," and in Jude 24, "Now unto him that is able to keep you from falling."

Often we spend more time in the Christian life calling the

wrecker than we do learning how to keep life's car on the road. There seems to be something in all of us that wants to go off the road.

One day a pilot was explaining to me the difference between a fixed-wing aircraft and a helicopter. He described the different dynamics of both craft by saying, "A fixed-wing aircraft wants to fly. A helicopter wants to crash."

If we are honest with ourselves, we'll admit that there is something inside us that wants to crash. Even when a person is born again, this fatal attraction continues to be a problem.

There's a text that explains how it works: "But every man is tempted, when he is drawn away of his own lust, and enticed. Then when lust hath conceived, it bringeth forth sin: and sin, when it is finished, bringeth forth death" (James 1:14, 15).

The bottom line is that the devil is continuously trying to connect with that aspect of us that the Bible calls "the man of sin." In electrical terms, you could say that he's trying to complete the circuit of evil from the outside to the inside. For this reason Paul declared that he had to die daily (1 Corinthians 15:31). And in Romans 7 and 8 he explains that it's only through the indwelling of the Holy Spirit that we're able to have victory.

In the Lord's Prayer Jesus teaches us to pray, "Lead us not into temptation, but deliver us from evil."

I used to have a problem with that concept, because it sounds as though Jesus is saying that God is the one who tempts us. Of course that can't be true. God would never tempt us to do evil. The Scripture is clear: "Let no man say when he is tempted, I am tempted of God: for God cannot be tempted with evil, neither tempteth he any man" (James 1:13).

I did my homework on this and discovered that in the Bible the word for "tempt" is the same as the one used for "to try" or "to test." I discovered biblical references stating that God indeed tried or tested individuals on occasion. But I also learned that the devil often tries or tests us. In one sense of the word, we could say that we are "tempted" (tested) by both God and Satan. There is, of course, a huge difference in the perspective of the testing.

When God tests us, He never uses evil to do it. And the tests He permits to come upon us are meant to develop strength of character and are ultimately for our salvation. The tests that Satan brings are always to weaken us and to try to cause us to renounce our salvation.

When we understand that difference, we can truly pray, "Lead us not into temptation," because the next phrase makes it clear: "but deliver us from the evil one" (Matthew 6:13).

But we're still left with the question Why should we be asking God not to lead us into situations in which we are enticed to do evil? As we learned from the text in James, God doesn't do that. So what's the point? Just this—when we pray not to be led into temptation, we are, in effect, affirming our intention to not needlessly expose ourselves to that which would cause us to sin. It's declaring our desire that God help us to stay far away from Satan's traps.

Unfortunately we are often not consistent in our prayers in this respect. Many of us suffer needlessly because we place ourselves in harm's way and in doing so have continued to make ourselves vulnerable to attack by the father of all terrorists.

In the weeks and months after September 11, 2001, measures were taken to make it extremely difficult for terrorists to highjack another plane. Not that it would be impossible for this ever to happen again, but as weaknesses in the system were identified, steps were taken that would make it much more difficult to repeat the disaster.

I was traveling; I don't remember exactly where or when. Trips seem to blur into one another and pretty well become generic. I do remember, however, that after I had preached, my colleagues brought me back to the motel around 5:30 p.m. Traveling can be fun until it comes to the evening, when I'm accustomed to being home.

By 6:30 I'd had a light supper; and because it was too early to go to bed, I decided to spend the next few hours watching television. Later when I had taken my shower, as is my custom, I knelt down to pray.

It can be curiously enlightening when we actually listen to our own prayers as we are praying. That night I was praying pretty much the usual bedtime prayer. About halfway through the prayer, I stopped. Because as I listened to myself, I realized I was contradicting myself, and I couldn't go on.

I heard myself pray that the Lord would make me like Jesus and that He would forgive the pride, selfishness, bitterness, lust, and lack of self-control in my life. You might be thinking, *So what's wrong with that?*

What was wrong was what I had been doing for the past two or three hours. Now, I wasn't watching HBO or pay-per-view movies. I had been watching whatever was on the network channels and considered "family entertainment." But the programs had been laced with the usual selfishness, pride, bitterness, and lust, to say nothing of the lack of self-control. There I was, being entertained by watching the actors simulate the very things for which Christ died, and then a few minutes later I was praying for the fruit of the Spirit! Could anything be more inconsistent?

Some would beg to differ with me; but I believe that television as watched by the average Christian is incompatible with all that we are praying the Holy Spirit will do in our lives.

Do I mean to say that we shouldn't watch TV?

I didn't say that. I'm simply sharing an experience that I had. You see, that night it occurred to me that I needed to bring my life up to the level of my prayers, that I couldn't have it both ways. It was clear to me then and is clear now that I was praying one thing and doing another.

Long ago, that night in Gethsemane, Jesus warned His disciples that they should pray, or else they would enter into temptation. And sure enough, down they fell. It wasn't that they didn't love Him. It was that they didn't understand how weak and vulnerable to temptation they were. And Jesus warns us too that, though the spirit might be willing, the flesh is weak.

When a person gives their life to Jesus and is born again, Paul describes them as being a spiritual baby, and that means weak and vulnerable. A person who is born again must be vigilant that their old experience with the man of sin not be allowed to renew old friendships with the ways of the world, whether they are real or make-believe. Should this happen, we are on the road to falling into sin, because we're "drawn aside of our own lust and enticed" (see James 1:14). In effect, we're setting ourselves up to be tempted, and when we do, our chances of falling are greatly enhanced.

There's an old saying: "You can't keep the birds from flying over your head, but you can keep them from nesting in your hair."

Victory over sin must begin with victory over temptation, and victory over temptation begins with prayer—a prayer in which we express to our heavenly Father that we will not needlessly expose ourselves to evil in its many shapes and sizes.

Our flesh is weak. Romans 7:18 says, "In me . . . dwelleth no good thing." We cannot needlessly make ourselves available to temptation and expect that we will never pay a price. If we put our hand in the fire, we shouldn't be surprised if we get burned.

Experience has taught us that we can be blindsided. Just when we realize that the devil is attacking from the east, he comes to us from the west. But as we grow in grace we will begin to recognize, from both within ourselves and outside ourselves, what we need to look out for. Sadly, some Christians are like the old-timer who said, "Too soon old and too late smart."

Could it be that although we claim we are praying to overcome temptation, we are often praying too late? My mother taught me to pray, and for that I will forever be grateful. She taught me to pray before I went to bed at night. It was many years later when I learned that an even more essential prayer of the day is the prayer we pray when we begin the day.

With tongue in cheek I often tell a congregation that the prayer at the end of the day can be the loser's prayer—the damage has already been done! It's the prayer in the morning that is a winner's prayer, because it's the prayer in which, with all our hearts, we put ourselves on the Lord's side.

When we pray, "Lead us not into temptation," it's another way of saying, "Today, Lord, we will not needlessly expose ourselves to evil." Friend, it is time that we brought our lives up to the level of our prayers. You have heard it said, "Put your money where your mouth is." I realized in the motel that evening that I couldn't have it both ways—I couldn't pray one way and live another.

Temptation is a reality. Jesus was tempted, and we are too. We greatly multiply our sorrow when we are not careful to avoid the things that, linking up with our weaknesses, may contribute to our fall.

I remember having to remind our children not to play in the street. Is playing in the street dangerous? Technically, no. It is the cars that travel in the streets that make it dangerous. In the Christian life there are many things that in and of themselves may be lawful, but they are not expedient. It was not unlawful for Eve to go to the tree of knowledge of good and evil, but it wasn't expedient. In the Christian journey experienced travelers know the dangers. They know their own weaknesses and are careful to avoid the needless risk that can result in sorrow and remorse.

Prayer is the process by which we keep ourselves alert to the potential for temptation and sin. If it's not already your custom, try giving your heart to Jesus the first thing in the morning. This will give you direction and purpose for the day. But remember, Jesus tells us not only to pray but to watch and pray. Later in the day, if unforeseen temptation appears in our path, we will discern the danger; and as we call out to God for deliverance we will experience the joy that comes from being overcomers.

Points to Consider

1. God allows trials to come into our lives. Their purpose is always to strengthen us.
2. The trials that the devil brings into our lives have as their purpose the destruction of our faith.

IF WITH ALL YOUR HEART

Some Things to Pray About

1. That the Lord, through His Word, will show us where we are subjecting ourselves needlessly to Satan's temptations.
2. That the trials through which we must pass will bring us closer to Jesus.

CHAPTER 8

HOW TO SHORT-CIRCUIT YOUR PRAYERS

G od's love is unconditional simply because that's the way He is. His relationship (interaction) with those He loves, however, is conditional. There are many texts that could illustrate this point, but two that we easily recognize are John 1:12 and Revelation 3:20:

John 1:12: "But as many as received him, to them gave he power to become the sons of God, even to them that believe on his name."

Revelation 3:20: "Behold, I stand at the door, and knock: if any man hear my voice, and open the door, I will come in to him, and will sup with him, and he with me."

In these days of the Internet and computer games, we know what interactive means. By their very nature, relationships between persons are interactive—if you do this, then I'll do that. We can't have a meaningful relationship with someone who refuses to have a relationship with us.

In the end, prayer is about having a relationship with Jesus, and this relationship must be

"If ye forgive men their trespasses, your heavenly Father will also forgive you: but if ye forgive not men their trespasses, neither will your Father forgive your trespasses."
—Matthew 6:14, 15.

based on interaction, not only between Jesus and us but also among one another.

Betty and I live in Florida. A short time after we moved into our house, I constructed a fountain in a corner of our backyard. It has a statuary of a girl pouring water into a birdbath, and from there the water cascades down into the pool where there are goldfish. (One morning Betty looked out the window and screamed. There on the edge of the pool was a great blue heron having a meal of hand-fed goldfish!)

Of course, in order to run the pump I had to install an underground electric line. Wherever electricity may come in contact with water, there must be what is called a ground fault breaker. This breaker is very sensitive and will stop the flow of current immediately if moisture gets into the line.

As I was considering this one day I realized that Jesus has, as it were, installed a ground fault breaker into our connection with Him in prayer, and if certain conditions exist, they will short-circuit our prayers.

Although God's love for us is unconditional, His ongoing relationship with us is predicated on one word: forgiveness. While He has promised that if we confess our sins, He is faithful and just to forgive us (1 John 1:9), He sets a ground fault breaker on our prayers when He says: "If ye forgive men their trespasses, your heavenly Father will also forgive you: *but if ye forgive not men their trespasses, neither will your Father forgive your trespasses*" (Matthew 6:14, 15).

Earlier in the Sermon on the Mount, from which this text is taken, Jesus had said: "If thou bring thy gift to the altar, and there rememberest that thy brother hath ought against thee; leave there thy gift before the altar, and go thy way; first be reconciled to thy brother, and then come and offer thy gift" (Matthew 5:23, 24).

Later in chapter 18 of this same book, Jesus drives the point home when He tells a story about a civil servant who owned the king a huge amount of money—10,000 talents. The talent was a weight, not a coin, and its value would depend on the purity of the precious metal used in the coinage. If the Greek silver talent were used, the 10,000 talents would amount to about $7.5 million. Jesus was illustrating that the sum was beyond human ability to pay. Back in those days it was not as easy as simply declaring bankruptcy. The king ordered that everything the man owned be liquidated and that he and his family be sold into slavery.

The man made the ridiculous promise that he would pay it all back; and though that would have been impossible, the king had compassion and forgave the debt. The man walked out the door and immediately met an acquaintance who owed him 100 pence. The denarius, or penny, was a silver coin worth the equivalent of 16 to 18 cents. The whole debt would be $16 to $18.

The unfortunate acquaintance couldn't pay that small amount, so the ungrateful servant of the king had him thrown in prison. When word of what had happened got back to the king, he changed his mind and had the ungrateful wretch put in jail until he could figure out how to pay what was really unpayable.

The message in these texts leaves no doubt that forgiving those who have wronged us is a condition for receiving God's forgiveness.

One Sabbath after I had preached a sermon on forgiveness, a woman approached me and said, "Pastor, I had some problems with a friend, and I've forgiven her. But I don't think she has forgiven me."

I assured her, "That's good, sister; at least you have forgiven her. Now you can get on with your life."

"But Pastor," she insisted, "she hasn't forgiven me."

I tried again. "OK, I understand. But I'm glad that at least you have forgiven her."

She persisted, "But she hasn't forgiven me, and she's supposed to."

By now I was beginning to have my suspicions. I smiled and gently replied, "Sister, I suspect that you really haven't forgiven her yet."

She thought a moment and said over her shoulder as she walked away, "You're probably right."

This woman's attitude was obviously "I'll forgive you if you'll forgive me."

But the Word of God commands us to forgive regardless of the attitude of the other person. In some cases the other person may never forgive us. But that is their problem, not ours. The apostle Paul points us in the right direction when he writes, "If it be possible, as much as lieth in you, live peaceably with all men" (Romans 12:18).

Someone may ask, "Does forgiving mean that we must forget?" I will answer that with a yes and a no.

Yes, we forget in an emotional sense. When we forgive at the level of our emotions, the result is that there will be no place for revenge and the problem won't "eat" on us anymore.

On the other hand, inasmuch as God asks us to give unilateral forgiveness, this would not necessarily mean that we would forget. For example, when someone is nominated to be church treasurer and we are aware that they once had problems with honesty, it would not be vengeful to bring this up in the nominating committee.

Yet holding a grudge and harboring a spirit of revenge are incompatible with the spirit of prayer. On several occasions a sister shared with me that she held a grudge against a sibling. I tried repeatedly to point her to the gift of forgiveness that God so graciously promises to give us if we ask. At one point, almost in desperation, she wrote, "I can't seem to forgive my brother—this is going to destroy me." This story has a happy ending. A year later she e-mailed me that God had given her the victory.

There is a reason that God commands us to forgive those who have wronged us as a *condición previa* to His forgiving us. The way it works is if we have decided that someone has wronged us for whatever reason and we refuse to forgive, we will find that repentance of our own sins will be impossible. This is because as long as we feel justified in not forgiving others for what they've done to us, we will not recognize our own faults. And when this happens, we will continue to rationalize away our own sins.

I know what it's like to be full of bitterness and resentment.

As I mentioned earlier, I went through a career crisis, and when it was all said and done I had a new job and lived in another state.

HOW TO SHORT-CIRCUIT YOUR PRAYERS

Although I had a new job and a new place to live, I brought with me deep bitterness and resentment against those who I felt were responsible for what had happened to me.

Not long afterward, I was on a trip. One night as I was sleeping in the motel room, I suddenly awakened. Though it is only a foggy memory now, I was terrorized by what seemed to be the faces of demons beside my bed.

Looking back on the experience now, I cannot say whether what I saw was real or only a nightmare, but I remember that I began to cry out with fear. And as I cried I began to pray for my enemies by name and to ask God to forgive my bitterness and resentment.

God heard my cry and healed my spirit. But though He took away my bitterness, my prayer didn't reverse all that had happened to me. We need to recognize that forgiveness won't put us back where we left off, but it will make it possible for us to go forward from where we are.

Someone may wonder what to say when we pray for our enemies. I don't believe we're supposed to pray, "God, teach them a lesson for what they have done to me." That kind of prayer could serve as a smoke screen for continuing to be resentful. When I have prayed for those who I feel have wronged me, I simply ask that God will do for them and their children what I am praying He will do for me and mine.

A spirit of forgiveness and a willingness to be reconciled to those who have wronged us removes fear. When Jacob wrestled with the angel that night so long ago on the other side of the river Jabbok, he was full of fear. After his encounter with the angel that night, though he couldn't be sure what would happen when he met his brother, he wasn't afraid anymore because the Lord had given him a spirit of repentance and forgiveness.

When Jacob and Esau met that day after so many years of estrangement, they wept on each other's shoulders. There is no record of how they related to each other after that. We do know that Jacob went his own way (Genesis 33:17). Perhaps their lifestyles were so different that they never interacted again. A spirit of forgiveness may or may not mean that in the future there will be closeness. Birds of a feather flock together. Differences in lifestyle will affect fellowship.

In my life, forgiveness has not always meant that I have become buddies with those against whom I was so bitter, but it definitely changed my feelings toward them. Reconciliation is not a one-way street. We cannot be reconciled in the fullest sense of the word with someone who will not be reconciled with us. "A man that hath friends must shew himself friendly" (Proverbs 18:24).

Someone shared with me an experience she was having with her daughter-in-law. The woman had done all that she could to be nice, but it seemed that she was always being rebuffed. I counseled her to continue to do what she could to reach her daughter-in-law and not to react negatively to the way she was being treated. Experience teaches us that people will often have problems that baffle our best intentions. We soon learn that ultimately reconciliation is a two-way street whose foundation must be laid by the Holy Spirit working in *both* hearts.

I read once that our personal world has only about a dozen people in it. These are the people with whom we closely relate. They would include the members of our family and those with whom we associate most closely at work.

It is often easier to pray for an enemy in some far-off country than it is to pray for and forgive those with whom we live and work. The real testing ground of the Christian life is the family, and the cutting edge of our prayers must be in maintaining a spirit of forgiveness and doing all we can to get along.

Too often we discover that we are failing the Christian life not at the level of advanced studies, but at the kindergarten level. We may pass some of the "big" tests but fail the "little" ones. You see, the Christian life is about basic things such as repentance and forgiveness, and when these are not happening, the family will be affected.

I believe this chapter on forgiveness is the most important one in the book, because it takes a willingness to forgive to literally get our prayers off the ground. The text that drives the point home is 1 John 2:9, which says, "He that saith he is in the light, and hateth his brother, is in darkness." A refusal to forgive those who have wronged us is a short-circuit to prayer.

I've noticed through the years that my relationship with God and my relationship with my wife are closely related. When things are not as they should be with God, it affects my relationship with Betty; and when things are not quite as they should be with Betty, it affects my relationship with God. Inasmuch as no human has seen God, the only way that we can know we love God is by demonstrating His love to each other (1 John 4:12). No wonder Scripture says, "If a man say, I love God, and hateth his brother, he is a liar: for he that loveth not his brother whom he hath seen, how can he love God whom he hath not seen?" (1 John 4:20).

A little boy came home from school one day, and his mother asked him what he had learned. He said that he had learned a prayer. When asked what it was, he said, "We learned to pray, 'Father, forgive us our trash baskets as we forgive those who put their trash in our baskets.'"

The result of our prayers must first and foremost be forgiveness and where possible reconciliation. The forgiveness that God gives so freely to us must be passed on to those whose lives we touch and whose lives touch ours. We must trash those feelings of revenge and bitterness.

By now you may be thinking, *Pastor O'Ffill, I know what you say is true. I've tried, but I just can't seem to forgive.* Friend, there's hope for us. While we were yet His enemies, our heavenly Father sent His Son to die for us. And if we will simply confess our bitterness and resentment and from the heart ask Him to give us His own spirit of forgiveness, He will. In fact, He will do it for you right now as you read these words.

As you look into your life, don't look far away or long ago. Start with the obvious right where you are now. The people against whom we often have the most bitterness tend to be members of our own families. It could even be your husband or wife, or maybe your mother or father.

If you know that you have bitterness and resentment in your heart toward someone, won't you let Jesus fix this short circuit so that by His Spirit He can light up your life? Your prayer for the gift of forgiveness may not at this moment change the heart of the one who has wronged you, but it will change your heart right now.

You may not be able to take up where you left off in your relationship with the other person, but you will be free to go on with a new kind of relationship and without the crushing emotional weight of the past.

When you do this, you will be able to say with the apostle Paul, "Brethren, I count not myself to have apprehended [arrived]: but this one thing I do, forgetting those things which are behind, and reaching forth unto those things which are before, I press toward the mark for the prize of the high calling of God in Christ Jesus" (Philippians 3:13, 14).

Points to Consider
1. Bitterness and resentment are a short circuit to effective prayer.
2. Often those against whom we have bitterness and resentment are closest to us.

Some Things to Pray About
1. That God will give us the wonderful gift of forgiveness for those who have wronged us.
2. That we will be able to learn how to pray even for those who hate us.

SAY "PRETTY PLEASE"

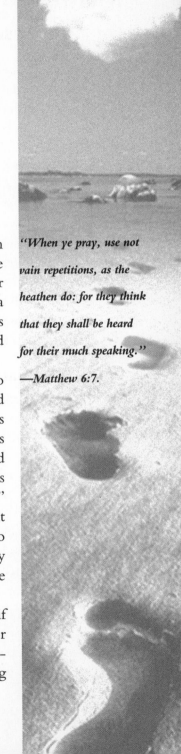

"When ye pray, use not vain repetitions, as the heathen do: for they think that they shall be heard for their much speaking."
—Matthew 6:7.

I s God waiting for us to pray a certain prayer in a certain way before He will answer our request? I remember that when, as a child, I would ask a playmate for a favor, they would sometimes reply, "Say 'Please.'" I would say "Please," and then they would insist, "Say 'Pretty please.'"

When we were in grade school we used to play a game called "Mother, may I?" We would first choose a "mother," and then the rest of us would line up at the starting line. The goal was to see who could reach "mother" first. The child whose turn it was to be "mother" would tell us by turns that we could take "five butterfly steps" or "three baby steps," or perhaps "two giant steps" toward her. Woe be to the person who went forward without first asking, "Mother, may I?" That unfortunate player had to go back to the starting line.

When you pray, have you ever wondered if there is an equivalent of "Mother, may I?" or "Pretty please?" before God will answer? In recent years the trend has been toward making

IF WITH ALL YOUR HEART

prayer a technique. Saying certain words in a certain way at a certain place has been purported to bring the best results.

Someone placed a weekly ad in a local newspaper that read: "St. Jude Novena: May the Sacred Heart of Jesus be adored, glorified, loved, and preserved throughout the world now and forever. Sacred Heart of Jesus, pray for us. St. Jude, Worker of Miracles, pray for us. St. Jude, Helper of the Hopeless, pray for us. Amen. Say this prayer nine times each day for nine days, then publish and your prayers will be answered. It has never been known to fail. Thank you, St. Jude."

During part of our ministry we lived in Southern Asia. Once I saw flags flying from the tops of hills all around a certain town. We were informed that these were Buddhist prayer flags. Prayers were written on pieces of cloth and then mounted as flags on poles. The idea was that as the wind blew across the flags, the prayers were carried to heaven. This same religion also has prayer wheels that are twirled around and around to repeat the prayer.

In Islam the ideal is to pray five times a day facing toward Mecca, and for best results the prayers must be in Arabic.

Nearer home, a few years ago a man named Bruce Wilkinson wrote a book about prayer that sold millions of copies. In *The Prayer of Jabez,* the author shared a little-known prayer from the Bible that he recommended should be repeated word for word. He claimed that he has prayed this same prayer for 30 years and that it has revolutionized his life and ministry.

The prayer is literally a four liner and is recorded in 1 Chronicles 4:10:

"Oh that thou wouldest bless me indeed,
    and enlarge my coast,
  and that thine hand might be with me,
  and that thou wouldest keep me from evil,
    that it may not grieve me."

It is not my purpose in this chapter to denigrate those who may have found that this prayer or any other prayer was a blessing to them; however, inasmuch as this book is about the meaning of prayer, I believe an issue we must resolve is whether or not Scripture recommends that we use a particular formula when we pray.

Before we discuss this, it is important to bear in mind that just because a particular technique or teaching has been a blessing to one does not necessarily make it so for everyone. Even if the prayer is sincere, it may not be a model prayer for everyone else. In the case of the prayer of Jabez, the author believes that his application of this prayer must be universal, because it is based on his own experience and the experience of thousands of others.

Friend, in everything having to do with matters in which truth and error struggle for the hearts of men and women, it is essential to remember that our faith must not be founded on the testimonies or the subjective experiences of others. Our faith must be totally founded in Scripture.

Wilkinson makes his claims for the prayer of Jabez based on his own manner of interpreting the verse and does not substantiate his exegesis of the text from other Scripture. If we could have asked Jabez what he meant to say, he very well could have replied, "I just wanted more land."

It is interesting to note that the prayer of Jabez is not mentioned again after 1 Chronicles 4. David didn't write a psalm about it. Though Paul calls on us to pray without ceasing, he never mentions Jabez's prayer. And of course when the disciples asked Jesus to teach them to pray, He didn't reference it.

The fact is, nowhere in Scripture is there a call for repetitive prayers. Nowhere are we commanded to repeat someone else's prayer other than our own. Some claim that repetitive prayers were used in the early Christian church, but there is no evidence that this was a widespread practice until the church became Romanized centuries later.

The prayer of Jabez is recommended as a *strategy* for sustaining a blessed life. Wilkinson issues a challenge: "Make the Jabez prayer for blessing part of the daily fabric of your life. To do that, I encourage you to follow unwaveringly the plan outlined here for the next 30 days. By the end of that time, you'll notice significant changes in your life, and the prayer will be on its way to becoming a treasured, lifelong habit."

It is interesting to compare the prayer of Jabez with the Lord's Prayer: "Our Father which art in heaven, Hallowed be thy name. Thy kingdom come. Thy will be done in earth, as it is in heaven. Give us this day our daily bread. And forgive us our debts, as we forgive our debtors. And lead us not into temptation, but deliver us from evil: For thine is the kingdom, and the power, and the glory, for ever. Amen" (Matthew 6:9-13).

While the prayer of Jabez has been recommended as a prayer formula, Jesus' model prayer is not intended to be a formula prayer but a model prayer. Jesus did not say, "Pray these precise words for 30 days," but "After this manner pray."

Prayer formulas can never match up to a heart-to-heart conversation with God. God doesn't want us to pray as robots. Jesus likened meaningless repetition to the prayer of the Gentiles (Matthew 6:7).

Christian prayer must not be confused with magic, which is an attempt to manipulate a power source for one's own ends. The true God cannot be manipulated or controlled. When prayer is reduced to techniques or formulas, a magical predisposition is in evidence. From the perspective of the magician, God is either an impersonal power that can be laid hold of by artful technique or a deus ex machina brought in as a last resort to solve a problem. The magician conceives of a god who can be made to do our bidding and who can be turned on or off like an electric current. The belief that the mere repetition of a prayer has automatic efficacy has more in common with magic than with biblical faith.

From time to time people have asked me what I think about asking God for signs. There are two ways to look at it. One way is to ask God for spiritual discernment so that we can see the signs of His working in our lives. The other is to put God to the test. Gideon tested God when he demanded particular signs as the condition for obeying the divine commandment. He first asked that the fleece of wool on the threshing floor be covered with dew even though the ground might be dry. When he arose the next morning, he was able to wring enough dew from the fleece to fill a bowl with water (Judges 6:36-38). Then he demanded another sign, that the fleece be dry while the ground be covered with dew. By making these demands, Gideon must have been aware that he was provoking God, because he prayed, "Let not Thine anger be hot against me" (verse 39).

Scripture calls us to walk by faith and not by sight (2 Corinthians 5:7). To ask for a sign may very well be an attempt to dictate the way in which God answers our prayers, or even an attempt to escape obedience. People of faith may plead with God and even complain to Him, but they do not try to control God. It is one thing to try to persuade God; it is quite another to try to manipulate Him.

The Israelites in the wilderness "tested God in their heart" by demanding the food they craved (Psalm 78:18, NKJV). God gave it to them, but the price they paid was in the death of thousands. Later, in the New Testament, we read that Zacharias (John the Baptist's father) asked for a sign (Luke 1:18-22), and he was struck dumb.

Demanding signs from God as a condition for our faithfulness is usually inspired not by faith but rather by doubt. Calvin rightly remarked, "If you doubt, you do not pray." Rather than ask for signs, we should follow this counsel: "Delight thyself also in the Lord; and He shall give thee the desires of thine heart. Commit thy way unto the Lord; trust also in him; and he shall bring it to pass" (Psalm 37:4, 5).

Though we should not demand signs of our own choosing, it is appropriate to pray that we discern the signs, showing that God is already working in our lives. "And this shall be a sign unto thee from the Lord, that the Lord will do this thing that he hath spoken" (Isaiah 38:7).

David prayed, "Shew me a token for good; that they which hate me may see it, and be ashamed: because thou, Lord, hast helped me, and comforted me" (Psalm 86:17). In this prayer David was asking for spiritual insight in order to discern the working of God in his life.

What shall we say, then, about asking for signs? Maybe it's not a good habit. What shall we say about looking for indications of His providence? Good idea!

I once read a sermon written by A. W. Tozer in which he asks why God should be more willing to answer prayers offered at 3:00 in the morning than those offered at 5:00 in the afternoon. I hadn't thought about that before. But just as we may tend to believe that there is a preferred set of words to use when we pray, we may also think that if God is going to take us seriously, we must pray all night.

While Jesus often did pray all night, and many great men and women of faith have done the same, is an all-night prayer session necessary to get God's attention?

I have not been able to find a text that teaches we must pray for a certain amount of time and at a certain time of day before God will answer our prayers.

There can be no doubt that wonderful blessings result from all-night prayer meetings. Whenever we gather in His name, He has promised to be present. Yet we must be aware that God does not work just 9:00 to 5:00, neither do we reach Him more effectively on the night shift. He is open to hear our prayers 24/7. While an all-night prayer session can be a wonderful blessing to those who participate, it is not a requirement to reach the heart of God. God is listening whenever we seek Him with all our heart.

There may be a feeling on the part of some that God favors the prayers of some over the prayers of others. Though doubtless there are those who give themselves often to prayer (we call them "prayer warriors"), it must not be concluded that these individuals have greater influence with God. Prayer is for everyone, from the first lispings of a child to the dying cry, "Lord, be merciful to me, a sinner."

Consider the listing of the gifts of the Spirit. "For to one is given by the Spirit the word of wisdom; to another the word of knowledge by the same Spirit; to another faith by the same Spirit; to another the gifts of healing by the same Spirit; to another the working of miracles; to another prophecy; to another discerning of spirits; to another divers kinds of tongues; to another the interpretation of tongues . . .

And God hath set some in the church, first apostles, secondarily prophets, thirdly teachers, after that miracles, then gifts of healings, helps, governments, diversities of tongues" (1 Corinthians 12:8-28).

Did you notice that missing in this list is the gift of prayer? The reason is obvious. Prayer is not a gift given to a special few. We are *all* called to pray. There is the danger that prayer become merely a "department" of the church or be perceived as something for a favored few.

We must not allow ourselves to think that our prayers are somehow inferior because we do not know how to offer "beautiful prayers." We can be inspired by eloquence and articulation, but we must not feel inadequate because we use simple words.

Prayer is not about time, though it takes time to pray. Prayer is not about words, though our thoughts are expressed in words. Prayer is, first and foremost, opening our hearts to God. His heart is already open to us. God calls us all to pray. If we can think, we can pray; true prayer springs from the heart.

Sometimes we don't know what to say, and this is understandable. There is an old story of the little boy who, when he knelt to pray, repeated the ABCs. When he was finished, he told his mother that he didn't know what to say and so he was going to let God put his letters into words.

Sometimes when I pray, my heart is so heavy I don't know what to say. Life can be so complicated and our burdens almost more than we can bear. But not to worry. The Lord knew it would be this way, and so we have the promise: "Likewise the Spirit also helpeth our infirmities: for we know not what we should pray for as we ought: but the Spirit itself maketh intercession for us with groanings which cannot be uttered" (Romans 8:26).

Someone has suggested that it is not the geometry of our prayers (how long they are), or the arithmetic of our prayers (how many they are), or the rhetorical expression of our prayers (how beautiful they are), or the logical exposition of our prayers (how argumentative they are or how loud they are).

IF WITH ALL YOUR HEART

Don't worry if your prayer is stammering and your language loose. Just as a mother understands the first lispings of her baby, so God understands your prayers.

As you have read this chapter, you may be saying, "Pastor O'Ffill, you have just messed up my prayer life." If I have, I apologize. It wasn't my purpose to put anyone or anything down. If you are a prayer warrior who prays the Jabez prayer, asks for signs, and prays all night, God bless you, and I'm thankful for you. The point of this chapter is simply to reassure you that if you don't happen to do those things in that way and at that time, you don't need to worry that you are a spiritually lesser life form and that your prayers to God don't count.

Prayer is deeper than words. Prayer is an attitude of the heart. Words don't mean nearly as much to God as does the cry of the heart. In order for prayer to be real, it must be a matter of the heart. And if with all our heart we truly seek Him, we will surely find Him.

Points to Consider

1. There are no magic prayers that must be learned before God will hear and answer us.
2. Though God will sometimes give a sign to show us that He is leading us, generally it is not wise to ask Him for a sign.

Some Things to Pray About

1. That we will trust God although we cannot see what lies ahead.
2. That we will believe He hears us as much as anybody else when we pray with all our hearts.

SHALL WE
EXPECT A MIRACLE?

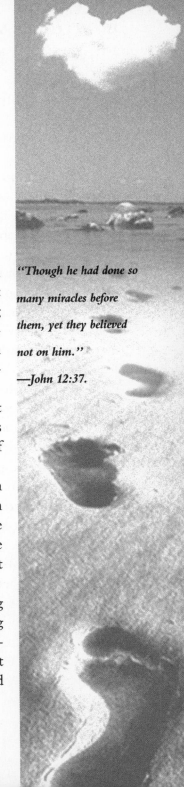

I t's easy to feel you have faith when you're sick and ask for healing and it comes; but when you ask for healing and it doesn't come, it may be difficult to believe in the power of prayer. More than one person has confessed, "I have stopped praying because God obviously isn't listening."

Author W. Somerset Maugham came to that conclusion as a little boy who stuttered. His Methodist uncle often talked about the power of prayer, so the boy decided to pray for healing.

One night before he went to bed, Maugham asked God to set him free from what was to him an embarrassing humiliation. As he prayed, he imagined how wonderful it would be in the morning when he could show his classmates that he could speak as well as they.

He fell into a hopeful sleep. In the morning he dressed quickly, ran downstairs, and, entering the kitchen where his parents were eating breakfast, blurted out, "Good m-m-m-morning." At that moment something in his soul died, and Somerset Maugham stopped praying.

"Though he had done so many miracles before them, yet they believed not on him."
—John 12:37.

IF WITH ALL YOUR HEART

Do miracles occur as a result of prayer? The answer is yes. Should we expect a miracle? This will be the subject of this chapter. Let's begin by defining a miracle as an event inexplicable by the laws of nature.

In Scripture there are, of course, wonderful examples of miracles that came in answer to prayer. Prayer opened the Red Sea. Prayer brought water from the rock and bread from heaven. Prayer made the sun stand still. It brought fire from heaven on Elijah's sacrifice; it protected Daniel in the lions' den and the three Hebrews in the fiery furnace.

The Gospels and the book of Acts are full of stories of miracles performed by Christ and His disciples.

Miracles did not stop with the apostles. Through the years there have been undeniable miracles. In my own ministry I remember the time a young wife came to me after a meeting. She explained that she desperately wanted a child. The doctors had examined her and advised her that this could never happen.

The young woman decided that this situation called for a miracle, so she began to pray. Nothing happened. She prayed with tears and fasting. Still nothing. Now she came to me, asking me to pray for her.

I asked if it ever occurred to her that maybe she was trying to force God to do a miracle. I suggested that probably what she needed to do was to go home and ask God to forgive her bad attitude and commit herself to His apparent will. And so we prayed together. I didn't see her again for about a year.

One day a young mother I didn't recognize walked up to me after a meeting carrying a baby. She promptly put the baby into my arms and told me who she was and how she had gone home that night after our prayer and, in tears, asked God to forgive her for trying to force Him to do as she wanted. She then committed the whole matter to Him. She told me she conceived the next day!

On another occasion a minister reminded me that one summer there was a severe drought during camp meeting time. Though I had forgotten the incident, he told me that I asked the people to join together in earnest prayer. We did, and it rained. The drought was broken.

Another time thousands of acres were on fire. It was also camp meeting time. The treasurer of a local church shared that her house was in the direct path of the fire. All the church financial records were inside her home. We joined hands in prayer. Later I received a card from her. It was good news. The fire was turned back, and her home was spared.

Scripture indicates that miracles will play an important part in last-day events. But it warns that there will also be miracles performed by demons. "For they are the spirits of devils, working miracles, which go forth unto the kings of the earth and of the whole world, to gather them to the battle of that great day of God Almighty" (Revelation 16:14).

One day I decided to type the word "miracle" into one of the search engines on the Internet. One site that came up was sponsored by a person who offered himself as a lecturer to speak on angels, UFOs, crop circles, healing crosses, Buddhist miracles, and the image of the Hindu elephant god that drank milk.

These kinds of supposed miracles may seem "far out," but what about the one in which more than 300 people at the Toronto Airport Christian Fellowship claim they have received gold fillings in their teeth as an answer to prayer? They say that this miracle is a fulfillment of the promise in Psalm 81:10: "I am the Lord thy God, which brought thee out of the land of Egypt: open thy mouth wide, and I will fill it."

A well-known author of a popular prayer bestseller has suggested that if we are praying correctly, we can expect a miracle every day. If this were possible, it could present a problem—because if miracles became commonplace, they wouldn't be miracles anymore.

Certainly Jesus' ministry was replete with miracles, from His first miracle of changing water to wine until He healed the high priest's servant's ear in the garden of Gethsemane. And along the way He healed countless incurable diseases and even raised the dead. He told His disciples that they would do even greater things than He did, and the book of Acts documents that they did, to the point that people were even sending around pieces of cloth the disciples had touched or hoping that a disciple's shadow would fall on them.

Will there be miracles in our time? The answer is yes. If that is the case, shall we expect a miracle on demand? Here is where we must be cautious.

A study of the miracles recorded in Scripture will bear out that miracles were never done just for the sake of doing a miracle. There was always a larger purpose involved. This must have been true, because all who were miraculously healed—and even raised from the dead—later died. Though the miracles had short-term medical benefits, their true significance can be appreciated only in their long-term implications.

Even the short-term results of miracles were not always positive. When Jesus fed the 5,000, the people saw a solution to their food budget problem and wanted to make Him king. When Jesus reached the end of His earthly ministry and was brought before Herod, the ruler was interested in only one thing: seeing this man he had heard so much about perform a miracle.

Miracles in and of themselves may confirm faith, but they will rarely create faith. There is a story in John 4:46-48 in which Jesus revealed the true motives of a man who had asked Him to heal his son. Apparently the man had decided he would test Jesus, and if Jesus passed the test, he would be a believer. "So Jesus came again into Cana of Galilee, where he made the water wine. And there was a certain nobleman, whose son was sick at Capernaum. When he heard that Jesus was come out of Judaea into Galilee, he went unto him, and besought him that he would come down, and heal his son: for he was at the point of death. Then said Jesus unto him, Except ye see signs and wonders, ye will not believe" (John 4:46-68).

Miracles that are meant to be a means to an end can soon become an end in themselves. The book of Acts tells the story of a man named Simon. Before he became a Christian, he had been a sorcerer. The people didn't know this about him and gave him credit for having the power of God. He was impressed when he saw the disciples doing miracles and at one point offered to pay them if they would give him the same kind of power. Whatever it was that they had, he wanted to buy a franchise. Miracles can, as it were, take on a life of their own.

Of all the types of miracles, the ones most requested usually have to do with physical healing. Thousands of people will come to see a faith healer. These healers guarantee that God promises physical healing based on the text in Isaiah 53:5: "With His stripes we are healed." Using this text as a promise of physical healing in the here and now is not valid. The verse refers to our transgressions and iniquities, and an honest reading in context makes it clear that these verses are a foreshadowing of the sacrifice of Jesus on the cross for our sins.

Popular faith healers are quick to point out that if a healing doesn't occur, it is because the disappointed petitioner didn't have enough faith. I was talking with the wife of a minister who shared with me that her mother was afflicted with a life-threatening disease. In her desperation the mother went to a faith healer. Later when she passed away, the members of the family were advised that the reason God hadn't healed her was that the family didn't have enough faith. Needless to say, they felt crushed.

A number of years ago the newspaper in the city where I live did an in-depth study of the healing ministry of one of America's premier faith healers. In all of their shadowing of the minister, they were not able to document one organic healing. When they confronted the minister with this, he shrugged and said it was because of a lack of faith.

One might wonder how these ministries are able to survive for so long. A physician once pointed out to me that in many cases of illness, a placebo is 37 percent effective. When I heard this, I could understand how the placebo phenomenon would provide sufficient "success stories" to keep a healing ministry alive.

IF WITH ALL YOUR HEART

Someone may ask, "But what about James 5:14, 15?", which reads: "Is any sick among you? let him call for the elders of the church; and let them pray over him, anointing him with oil in the name of the Lord: and the prayer of faith shall save the sick, and the Lord shall raise him up; and if he have committed sins, they shall be forgiven him."

There are several ways to look at these verses. The text is clear that the "Lord shall raise him up." It is probably safe to say that in the majority of the cases of anointing, the prayed-for person is not healed at the time and may even die. This cannot mean that the Scripture is deceiving us or, as is alleged by some, that the failure to get well is because of a lack of faith. Some feel that when the text says God will raise up the sick it means in His own time, but definitely when the trumpet sounds and the dead in Christ rise first.

Here is another application that is comforting and factors in the phrase "if he have committed sins, they shall be forgiven him." Let's say a person wanders away from the Lord, and now he is sick and in the last moments of his life. He calls for the elders, they anoint him with oil, and he recommits himself to the Lord. His sins are forgiven, and though he passes to his rest, he will be raised up in the last day.

There is a story in Matthew 20:1-15 about a man who hired people to work in his fields. Several times during the day he took men from the labor pool and, promising them a day's wages, put them to work. At the end of the day, no matter how long the men had worked, they were all paid the same.

I used to resent the concept of what we often call "deathbed conversions." I thought they weren't fair. Now I realize how gracious our heavenly Father is. He is not willing that any should perish. We who have worked through the "heat of the day" are privileged to have served. What a thrill to realize that whenever with all our heart we seek Him, even at the last moment of life, He is there to respond, and He will raise us up.

One day I was sitting at my dad's side. He had suffered a stroke, and Parkinson's disease was making his body stiff and rigid. As I looked at this man who had once been strong and handsome, tears came to my eyes. I thought, *God, is this our prize? Is this what we get?*

My dad spent nearly 40 years in the ministry. Through the years he baptized hundreds. Was this now his reward? Of course the answer is no. You see, there is no data to substantiate that those who have been faithful will not suffer and die. God used men and women throughout the ages to perform miracles, yet when many of them needed a miracle for themselves, it wasn't there.

The wages of sin is death. It is appointed to human beings once to die (Hebrews 9:27). Unless we survive until Jesus comes, we must one day pass over the Jordan. Though God has used miracles to protect and even to advance His truth, this is the exception rather than the rule.

What would happen if God always performed a miracle on demand? Would our personal commitment to Him grow, or would we try to exploit His power for our own purposes? After all, we do tend to pray for selfish reasons. "Ye ask, and receive not, because ye ask amiss, that ye may consume it upon your lusts" (James 4:3).

Should we then expect a miracle, or shouldn't we? If you mean the greatest miracle of all—a new heart—the answer is yes. Yet we must remind ourselves that flesh and blood will not inherit the kingdom of heaven. "Now this I say, brethren, that flesh and blood cannot inherit the kingdom of God; neither doth corruption inherit incorruption" (1 Corinthians 15:50). But we must also remember that while we are in this world, it is our lot to suffer, and no amount of prayer or faith will in every case take away our suffering. Yet we have the promise that "there hath no temptation [trial] taken you but such as is common to man: but God is faithful, who will not suffer you to be tempted above that ye are able; but will with the temptation also make a way to escape, that ye may be able to bear it" (1 Corinthians 10:13).

My niece's teen-age son was in a serious automobile accident. He suffered head injuries that put him in a coma for several weeks. As a family we drew together to support one another. For what did we pray? Of course we prayed that Kyle would be healed, but was that all we should pray for?

IF WITH ALL YOUR HEART

The greatest healing we all need as families is spiritual healing. As families we need to make our calling and election sure, to seek first the kingdom of God and His righteousness. Our extended family decided that in this time of crisis we would pray for more than Kyle's recovery. We prayed that God would use this accident to strengthen the family, and that as a result of this tragic event we would draw closer to Jesus and closer to each other. When tragedies happen, families sometimes fall apart and actually lose faith. We prayed that this wouldn't happen, but rather that this experience would be remembered as a time when Jesus would mean more to us than ever before. The Lord answered our prayers on both counts.

God will always be near us in sickness, sometimes by removing it and other times by giving us the strength to bear it. The prayer for healing, if offered from the heart, in faith, will be answered by God, but in His own way and time. God may well answer our prayers by saving our soul or healing our emotions, even though He may at times leave us in physical sickness for a while. But we know that He is not finished with us yet. He has gone to prepare a place for us, and through the Holy Spirit He is in this life preparing us to live there.

Healing is a gift of God. In the prayer for healing we are not to seek to manipulate the divine power. Healing, if it is going to be lasting, is brought about by the Spirit of God and not by the spiritual exercises of humanity.

Whether we are healed or not has nothing to do with whether we have found favor in God's sight. The case of Paul is classic. Rather than healing Paul of his affliction, God gave him grace to bear his infirmity. We would do well in times of sickness to remind ourselves, "For this thing I besought the Lord thrice, that it might depart from me. And he said unto me, My grace is sufficient for thee: for my strength is made perfect in weakness. Most gladly therefore will I rather glory in my infirmities, that the power of Christ may rest upon me. Therefore I take pleasure in infirmities, in reproaches, in necessities, in persecutions, in distresses for Christ's sake: for when I am weak, then am I strong" (2 Corinthians 12:8-10).

SHALL WE EXPECT A MIRACLE?

God answered a prayer for rain. He stopped a forest fire, and He gave a baby to a childless couple. But the most spectacular answer to prayer in my life was when one of my sons was delivered from alcohol and drug addiction.

God knows when a miracle is necessary for the advancement of His kingdom. There is always a danger that I want miracles for the advancement of my personal kingdom. As a minister I have a potential conflict of interest with God. The advancement of His kingdom can easily be a thinly veiled excuse for the advancement of my own selfish interests.

In the last days miracles are not a test of truth, and for that matter, they never were. From the time when the magicians in Pharaoh's court duplicated the miracles of Moses until today the forces of darkness have continued to perform miracles to provide legitimacy to error and evil.

Will the Lord perform miracles in answer to our prayers? The answer is yes. Shall we expect a miracle? The answer is probably no. God will choose the time and the place of miracles, and they will always be for the long view of the advancement of His kingdom until that time when the trumpet will sound and the dead in Christ shall rise first, and He will wipe away all tears from our eyes and make all things new.

Points to Consider

1. There is always the danger that we serve God for what we can get out of it.
2. The miracles that Jesus performed had implications that reached beyond this life alone.

Some Things to Pray About

1. That God will forgive us when we try to get Him to serve us rather than committing ourselves to serve Him, come what may.
2. That we will put the healing of our emotions and spiritual lives above all else.

CHAPTER 11

THE DEVIL MADE ME DO IT

"Heal the sick, cleanse the lepers, raise the dead, cast out devils: freely ye have received, freely give."

—*Matthew 10:8.*

Dick, how do you feel about exorcism?" It was the mid-1980s, and an old friend was asking me the question. He was a retired minister, and some years earlier we had worked together in another conference. I was some miles from home conducting revival meetings in his home church at the time of his question.

In those years exciting accounts abounded, such as the story of 50 or more demons being cast out of one person as a result of prayer. Books were written explaining the techniques that needed to be used. One set of instructions went something like this: "When helping others, challenge the right of the demons to come to the fore, order them to give you their names and what they were assigned to do. Once they have done this, you order them in the name of Jesus Christ to get out. They often yell and scream. Say to the demons, 'You can't do this to this person. In the name of Jesus Christ, you have got to stop, get out, and never return.' Order the captain of the assigned demonic garrison to step out of ranks, come forward, and stand to attention. . . . Demons are always harassing people, so beat them at their own game by hassling them back with Scripture. Irritate them till they can't stand it any longer and want to leave. They hate hearing about Jesus and how He has already defeated them. They won't go easily, but continue to hassle them in prayer until they leave. It will be a war of words, and they will fight to the very last, until Jesus Himself will make them go. . . . Call out the commander of the battalion and order all of them out, telling them that in the name of Jesus Christ you have power and authority over them."

There were reports of demons identifying themselves. When asked their names, some said that their name was Cookies; others were Mayonnaise, and still others had names more to be expected, such as Sex, Lying, and Criticism.

I like to consider myself open-minded and don't want to be guilty of quenching the Spirit. I told my friend that I did believe in exorcism. He continued, "There is a woman here tonight named Sarah [not her real name]. She has been having trouble with demons, and we have had several sessions with her. She seems to still have trouble, and we may need to have another prayer session with her. Would you be interested in accompanying us if we decide this is necessary?"

Without hesitation I replied, "Yes, I'd be interested."

I finished the week of meetings and returned to my hometown. A couple days later the phone rang. It was my pastor friend.

"Sarah is definitely having problems with demons again. We are going to pray for her at 11:00 tomorrow morning at my house. Can you come?"

My pulse quickened. "Yes, I'll be there."

I'd not had any direct experiences with demon possession since I had been overseas—the story I relate in the book, *Transforming Prayer*. Since there was currently so much interest in exorcism, I welcomed the opportunity to see for myself what was going on.

When I arrived, Bob and his wife met me at the door and soon introduced me to Sarah, a young woman of about 32. I asked Sarah how long she had been harassed by demons, and she related her problems as a single mother and the appearance of the symptoms that had led her to conclude she was being harassed by demons. After about 10 minutes, Bob suggested that we go to prayer.

Sarah lay down on the couch and closed her eyes. First we offered a prayer asking God to lead us, and then Bob's wife suggested we sing the "Battle Hymn of the Republic" (it had been recommended that this would help to cast out the demons). As we sang, Sarah's eyes blinked.

"There they are," whispered Pastor Bob. This was apparently a sign that the demons were manifesting themselves. Soon Bob began to pray again. This time Sarah interrupted him—or I should say the demons spoke through Sarah's mouth. Over the next hour and a half we sang, prayed, and interviewed the demons that apparently had chosen to manifest themselves.

I was deeply touched. The great controversy becomes real when one is actually talking with the forces of evil. I don't remember all the details or exactly how many demons were exorcised from Sarah that day. But I do remember that it was an experience that brought tears to my eyes, and as I drove back home that day I had become a believer.

Over the next weeks and maybe even months I would be called to go see Sarah again and again, because for some reason she couldn't seem to be set completely free from the spirits that were making her life difficult.

Things took a new turn one day as I knocked on the pastor's door yet another time. He met me with excitement in his voice. "You won't believe what is happening to Sarah. After we have had the prayers to cast out the demons, I will tell you."

He seemed so excited that I replied, "Why not tell me now?"

"Sarah," he informed me, "is getting messages from God."

A shiver went down my spine. "How can that be?"

Bob explained that after our most recent prayer session God had begun to dictate messages word by word to Sarah, and she had written them down. In fact, she had brought them with her that day for us to read.

From then on we would have special prayers to cast out Sarah's demons one day, and on the days when the demons were not harassing her, she would write messages that she claimed were being dictated to her by God.

Not only was this happening to Sarah, but across the country reports began to come in that numbers of people who had supposedly been demon-possessed were now claiming to receive messages from heaven.

I called a minister friend on the other side of the country who was known to be active in casting out demons and asked him what he thought about the "messages." He told me that he was keeping an open mind.

For me, it all came to an end one night shortly after midnight. We were praying for Sarah again. The demons were supposedly being cast out, but five minutes later they were back again. This was happening repeatedly in spite of our prayers and songs. Suddenly I blurted out, "This makes no sense."

"Quiet," said Pastor Bob, "the devil will hear you."

"I don't care. This is ridiculous."

With us that night was a fellow pastor who agreed with me, and so saying, we left and never went back to pray for Sarah. Pastor Bob and his wife were not daunted. They became even more involved in exorcism, and it wasn't long before his wife began to receive messages as well.

In due time Sarah moved away and got on with her life. The whole matter just faded away. She married and, as far as I know, lived happily ever after. I was informed years later that she was controlling her emotional condition with medication and was pretty well stabilized and living a normal life.

I do not relate this story to suggest that I don't believe in demon possession. I most assuredly do. But having said that, I must also state that I believe that much of what is going on, though in the devil's interest and though it furthers his kingdom, is probably not the result of his direct involvement. Rather it may well be the result of problems having to do with emotional or even psychological causes or simply the need to have something to blame. While I am not denying real demonic oppression, it seems strange that emotional states that are sometimes called demon possession can sometimes be calmed by the appropriate medication.

I was talking with a friend of mine who had been a member of a charismatic church. He related that whenever he seemed to be having problems in his life, some of his friends at church would suggest that maybe demons were behind his problems and that he ought to have them cast out. He would usually agree. As we talked about this, he confessed to me that he began to look at the experience as a kind of spiritual cleansing or emotional release and would get along just fine until the next time.

In some groups it is not uncommon for the praying one to suddenly begin addressing their words to the devil. They may say something such as "And now in the name of Jesus, we bind you, Lucifer, we cover you with the blood and command you to go to the pit." Then they will resume praying to God again. I was once with a group of evangelicals at a retreat. We sang a song that I hadn't heard before. The first verse was addressed to Jesus, and the second verse was addressed to the devil. The words of the verse rebuked him, bound him, and put him under the blood of Jesus.

Some time ago I attended a prayer conference led by a well-known evangelical who at the time was president of the World Prayer Conference. He informed us that during the next few years it was his intention to map the world for demons and discover the names of the devils that were in charge of particular areas of the planet. Some time later I received notice in the mail that this man was sponsoring a trip to the ruins of the temple of Diana of the Ephesians with the declared intention of casting out the demons that he believed dwelled there.

It is common for prayer groups to walk through neighborhoods in cities casting out the demons that supposedly are in charge there, and then they claim the area for Christ.

When Jesus sent the 70 on their missionary journey, they were given power over demons. When they returned they reported to Jesus, "Even the devils are subject to us through thy name" (Luke 10:17). There can be no doubt that casting out demons was an important feature of Christ's ministry on earth. The question that faces us as we study the subject of prayer is To what extent should we focus our prayers on what is now referred to as spiritual warfare?

In the early 1980s I was fascinated by the possibility of casting out demons. I began to focus more on doing battle with the devil than I did in looking to Jesus as the one who has broken the power of the enemy. When I was tempted, instead of praying, "Jesus, help me," I would pray, "Get thee behind me, Satan." I began to see a demon behind every tree.

There is a fascination that comes from doing battle against the devil, an adrenaline rush a cut above the warfare against one's own propensities and bad habits. From a purely excitement point of view, there is something to be said for being able to say "The devil made me do it" and then saying a prayer, binding the evil force, and casting him into the "pit."

I affirm the words of the apostle Paul, who declared: "For we wrestle not against flesh and blood, but against principalities, against powers, against the rulers of the darkness of this world, against spiritual wickedness in high places" (Ephesians 6:12). There are things that the devil will try to do in the life of the Christian that are not necessarily demon possession.

He will try to afflict us physically (2 Corinthians 12:7, Luke 13:16, and Acts 10:38).

He will try to incite fierce opposition to Christians and our message (Revelation 2:10).

He will try to create misunderstanding among fellow believers.

He will try to oppress the spirit, which may make the believer feel depressed, restless, and aimless.

He can inject irrational fear into our hearts.

He can inject unclean or confused thoughts into the believer's mind.

He can cause fellow workers to misunderstand the truth and oppose us in our work for the Lord (Matthew 16:23).

By deceit and counterfeit he leads multitudes into doctrinal error (Genesis 3:13; 2 Corinthians 11:3, 14, 15).

He can raise opposition to us on the basis of genuine human affection (Matthew 16:23; Mark 3:20, 21, 31-35).

These points being valid, the issue is not whether the Christian must do warfare against the devil. Rather, it's how this is best accomplished.

Jesus declared in John 12:31, "Now is the judgment of this world: now shall the prince of this world be cast out." On numerous occasions Jesus referred to Satan as the prince of this world. When Adam sinned, his place as the prince of this world was taken by Lucifer. Jesus, as the second Adam, came to dethrone the devil and has taken his place. "And the seventh angel sounded; and there were great voices in heaven, saying, The kingdoms of this world are become the kingdoms of our Lord, and of his Christ; and He shall reign for ever and ever" (Revelation 11:15).

Inasmuch as Jesus is now Lord of this world, when we are harassed by evil forces, it seems to me we should talk to Jesus about it. We have an intercessor who has overcome the devil, and in our battle against the flesh and the devil we do well to direct our prayers to Him who has already gained the victory.

Have you ever considered what would happen if suddenly the devil were no more? Would that be the end of our problems? Would sin suddenly disappear? What about death, war, and suffering? Though Satan is the original "dirty old man," at this stage in the world's history he is not the only one.

The Bible teaches that the human heart is desperately wicked: "The heart is deceitful above all things, and desperately wicked: who can know it?" (Jeremiah 17:9).

THE DEVIL MADE ME DO IT

Romans 7:18 says, "For I know that in me (that is, in my flesh,) dwelleth no good thing: for to will is present with me; but how to perform that which is good I find not."

Isaiah 55:8 declares, "'For my thoughts are not your thoughts, neither are your ways my ways,' saith the Lord."

Though the devil is making war with the people of God, and though he goes about like a roaring lion seeking whom he may devour, it is safe to say that evil is so engrafted into the hearts of human beings that if something were to happen to the devil, evil would continue to prosper (though obviously it would lose its coordination and its leadership).

Our greatest enemy is ourselves. The Bible often describes our nature as "the flesh":

"This I say then, Walk in the Spirit, and ye shall not fulfill the lust of the flesh. For the flesh lusteth against the Spirit, and the Spirit against the flesh: and these are contrary the one to the other: so that ye cannot do the things that ye would. Now the works of the flesh are manifest, which are these: Adultery, fornication, uncleanness, lasciviousness. . . . And they that are Christ's have crucified the flesh with the affections and lusts" (Galatians 5:16-24).

At one time you could find a popular little plaque on desks that read, "The devil made me do it." I am convinced that, though Satan is our implacable enemy, in terms of priority of our prayers we would do well to spend less time fighting the devil and more time dying to self and resisting the sins that come from inside us.

There can be no doubt that the devil is the enemy of our souls. But to focus on him can result in two things: (1) it can cause us to diminish our own responsibility, and (2) it can cause us to take our eyes off Jesus, from whom our victory is already won.

We can expect to be tempted and afflicted by Satan. Jesus was, and so was Job. Even though Job's afflictions could be directly attributed to demonic work, the issue through all of his trial was not whether he would exorcise the devil from his life but whether he would remain faithful to his God.

IF WITH ALL YOUR HEART

We are in a storm. Shall we fight the waves or shall we seek shelter from the one who is a shelter in the time of storm?

Points to Consider
1. Jesus has already gained victory over the devil. We need only ask Jesus to give us His victory.
2. Though we are in a battle with the forces of evil, we must place our emotional focus on Jesus.

Some Things to Pray About
1. That the Lord will impress us with our own responsibility for the things that we do.
2. That when we are tempted, we will cry out to Jesus for help.

CHAPTER 12

DOES IT HELP TO FAST?

I t was the season to do "Uplift." That is what they used to call Ingathering in Pakistan.

Over there it was not the custom to go door to door but rather to business and industry. I remember how impressed I was when a factory owner gave us the equivalent of $1,000.

We had been working since morning, and it was now noon. We hadn't packed a lunch, thinking we would buy something to eat along the way. What we had forgotten was that it was Ramadan, the month in which the Muslim world doesn't eat or drink between sunrise and sunset. We joked that though someday there would be a law against buying and selling, not being able to eat was a step beyond! But we learned that most Muslims are devout and careful to observe Ramadan, so we were careful the next time to pack our lunches.

Another time during Ramadan I was taking the "red eye" on Pakistan International Airlines. It was about 3:00 o'clock in the morning, and I was trying to snooze. Suddenly the lights came

"Therefore also now," saith the Lord, "turn ye even to me with all your heart, and with fasting, and with weeping, and with mourning: and rend your heart, and not your garments, and turn unto the Lord your God: for he is gracious and merciful, slow to anger, and of great kindness, and repenteth him of the evil."
—*Joel 2:12, 13.*

on, and the cabin attendants began to serve a full meal to the passengers. I wondered what was going on. We had not crossed any time zones. Then it occurred to me that this meal before sunrise would be the last meal of the day for all good Muslims until sunset.

In Islam there are three groups who are not required to fast—the very young, the old, and the sick. (One man confessed that he was "sick" every year for Ramadan.) For the Muslim, fasting serves many purposes. While the devout are hungry and thirsty, they are reminded of the suffering of the poor. Fasting is also an opportunity to practice self-control and to cleanse body and mind.

The Old and New Testaments include more than 100 references to fasting. In Scripture, if a feast signaled a celebration, fasting usually signified sadness. Moses passed 40 days in the mountain of the Lord without eating or drinking but was miraculously sustained. Jesus spent 40 days fasting and nearly perished as a result. In modern times one who was noted for fasting was Mahatma Gandhi, the father of modern India. He used fasting as a regular part of his spiritual life, but he also threatened to kill himself by fasting if his political demands were not met. We sometimes call this type of fast a "hunger strike."

Does it help to fast? If by that we mean, Do we have to go on a hunger strike to persuade God to answer our prayers? the answer is no. A fast is for our benefit, not for God's.

Although appetite is necessary for human existence, it was the hook the devil first used to separate man from his Creator. "And . . . the woman saw that the tree was good for food, and that it was pleasant to the eyes" (Genesis 3:6). Throughout history unbridled appetite has often kept people from a close relationship with God.

Esau sold his birthright for a bowl of lentils. Twice the children of Israel rebelled against God because of appetite. "And the children of Israel said unto them, Would to God we had died by the hand of the Lord in the land of Egypt, when we sat by the flesh pots, and when we did eat bread to the full; for ye have brought us forth into this wilderness, to kill this whole assembly with hunger" (Exodus 16:3).

"And the people spake against God, and against Moses, Wherefore have ye brought us up out of Egypt to die in the wilderness? for there is no bread, neither is there any water; and our soul loatheth this light bread" (Numbers 21:5).

Along with pride and too much free time, the people of Sodom are remembered as having "fullness of bread" (Ezekiel 16:49). Jesus was tempted to turn stones into bread, and He later reminded His disciples that eating and drinking to excess would be a characteristic of the last days (Matthew 24:38). Our Lord cautions that when there is a perceived delay in the coming of Christ, people will begin to "eat and drink, and to be drunken" (Luke 12:45).

This generation has a double major—sex and food. As a race we cannot exist without either, but when these God-given needs and drives become all-consuming, a genuine spirit of prayer is all but impossible. Though God has given us our bodies and planted within them certain basic instincts, we are required to keep the physical subservient to the spiritual. The body is to be our servant, not our master.

The Bible doesn't say that fasting must be a necessary practice of the believer, but it does recommend and encourage it. But the practice or nonpractice of fasting is a matter of complete liberty. Though Jesus didn't specifically command us to fast, He did correct its abuses.

"Moreover when ye fast, be not, as the hypocrites, of a sad countenance: for they disfigure their faces, that they may appear unto men to fast. Verily I say unto you, They have their reward. But thou, when thou fastest, anoint thine head, and wash thy face; that thou appear not unto men to fast, but unto thy Father which is in secret: and thy Father, which seeth in secret, shall reward thee openly" (Matthew 6:16–18).

We don't need to explain what He was trying to say. Unfortunately, in matters having to do with spiritual disciplines, we often don't do as He has asked.

There are several kinds of fasts. For the moment we will focus on the one that omits all food for a period of time. There are several important physical aspects that should be kept in mind:

1. If you are on regular medication, or have a regular medical condition, it is wise to obtain medical advice before entering into any fast that extends beyond a meal or two.

2. In the early period of a fast, you may experience unpleasant physical symptoms, such as dizziness, headache, or nausea. Do not allow physical discomfort to discourage you. After the first day or two, those unpleasant physical reactions usually subside.

3. Remember that hunger is partly a matter of habit. In the early stages of a fast, hunger will probably return at each normal mealtime. But if you hold out, the sensation of hunger will soon pass. Sometimes you can fool your stomach by drinking a glass of water instead of eating.

4. During a fast some people drink only water. Others take various kinds of fluid, such as fruit juices. You will need to work out something that is best for you.

5. Guard against constipation. Before and after fasting, it is important to choose meals that will help you in this respect.

6. Break your fast gradually. Begin with meals that are light and easy to digest. The longer you have fasted, the more careful you need to be about breaking your fast. If you eat too much after a fast, it can cause serious physical discomfort and nullify the benefits of the fast.

For years I had the habit of not eating from noon on Thursday until Friday evening. I did this primarily for health reasons, although there was a spiritual benefit.

Though fasting is not necessary as far as God is concerned, it can make a definite impact on our spiritual focus. While fasting serves to break down barriers in our carnal nature that stand in the way of the Holy Spirit, it should not be seen as a gimmick or a cure-all. God has made full provision for the total well-being of His people in every aspect of their lives, and fasting is only a part of the total provision.

Fasting can positively impact the prayer life, because it means that during the period without food we can focus on things spiritual. In its broadest sense fasting is laying aside every hindrance to prayer.

"Wherefore seeing we also are compassed about with so great a cloud of witnesses, let us lay aside every weight, and the sin which doth so easily beset us, and let us run with patience the race that is set before us" (Hebrews 12:1). Fasting is putting prayer first. Esther didn't eat food or drink water for three days (Esther 4:16).

The concept of fasting is something much deeper than simply going without food and devoting oneself to prayer. A true fast is moderation and self-denial, not only in regard to our appetites but in every aspect of our lives.

Joel 2:12, 13 is a call to fasting. "Therefore also now, saith the Lord, turn ye even to me with all your heart, and with fasting, and with weeping, and with mourning: and rend your heart, and not your garments, and turn unto the Lord your God: for he is gracious and merciful, slow to anger, and of great kindness, and repenteth him of the evil."

Notice that the call is not to stop eating but to stop sinning. Fasting, weeping, and mourning were to be outward indications of something that must go on in the heart.

Isaiah 58 describes two kinds of fasting. One is the kind that Jesus condemned in which a person would go through all the motions but they would be only mechanical—spirituality by the numbers. The Lord said, "Yet they seek me daily, and delight to know my ways, as a nation that did righteousness, and forsook not the ordinance of their God: they ask of me the ordinances of justice; they take delight in approaching to God. Wherefore have we fasted, say they, and thou seest not? wherefore have we afflicted our soul, and thou takest no knowledge? Behold, in the day of your fast ye find pleasure, and exact all your labours. Behold, ye fast for strife and debate, and to smite with the fist of wickedness: ye shall not fast as ye do this day, to make your voice to be heard on high" (Isaiah 58:2-4).

These verses describe a highly developed devotional life. The people are doing all the right things. Their prayer and fasting technique is exemplary. They wonder why it doesn't seem to be doing any good. The Lord tells them plainly. Down deep, their devotional life is really shallow. They are in effect doing all the right things for all the wrong reasons.

In verses 6 and 7 God tells them what a real fast is all about. "Is not this the fast that I have chosen? to loose the bands of wickedness, to undo the heavy burdens, and to let the oppressed go free, and that ye break every yoke? Is it not to deal thy bread to the hungry, and that thou bring the poor that are cast out to thy house? when thou seest the naked, that thou cover him; and that thou hide not thyself from thine own flesh?"

Though prayer and fasting can bring us closer to Jesus, we can do both and in effect be far from Him.

I hope that you are beginning see where I am coming from in this book. These days prayer and the devotional life is "in." Everybody who is anybody seems to be into prayer, which is good, but prayer must not be allowed to become a form. We can fast and pray and still not be in touch with God. In the verses above the people ask, "Haven't you noticed that we have been praying and fasting a lot?" The answer is, "That may be, but it seems to be only a form of godliness that has denied the power that was meant to come when with all our hearts we truly seek Him." As we will learn in future chapters, the purpose of prayer is a changed life.

Points to Consider
1. Fasting is not for God's sake, but for ours.
2. True prayer is not a technique.

Some Things to Pray About
1. That the Lord will give us the fruit of the Spirit, which is self-control.
2. That we may see that the changed life is the greatest miracle of all.

CAN PRAYER
MAKE YOU RICH?

If there was ever a time in which the behavior of our Lord bordered on the violent, it was when He threw the money changers out of the temple. He did this twice in His ministry. The first time He actually carried a little whip, probably made of some rope lying nearby. The second time was the week before His crucifixion, just after the triumphal entry.

"And they come to Jerusalem: and Jesus went into the temple, and began to cast out them that sold and bought in the temple, and overthrew the tables of the moneychangers, and the seats of them that sold doves; and would not suffer that any man should carry any vessel through the temple. And he taught, saying unto them, Is it not written, My house shall be called of all nations the house of prayer? But ye have made it a den of thieves" (Mark 11:15-17).

In a letter focused directly on poor widows and women struggling with financial troubles, a well-known television evangelist wrote an appeal. In it were included two pennies with the instructions:

"It is written, My house shall be called the house of prayer; but ye have made it a den of thieves."
—*Matthew 21:13.*

1. Take your personal prayer sheet and place the palm of your right hand over the two copper pennies.
2. Write down today's date in the box marked "today."
3. Be specific and write the miracle amount of money that you need.
4. Write down any other personal areas of need for which you are desperately desiring a miracle.
5. Finally, search your heart and write a check. Whatever you give, make it the best gift to Him that you possibly can.

The letter concluded by saying that the evangelist would instruct each prayer warrior who came in contact with the prayer request sheet to make sure they touched the same two coins the donor had touched. Next they would form a "prayer tunnel" of financial faith for the donor. The letter closed with the final appeal to "sow a seed out of your need."

This high-tech generation has learned that prayer can be an excellent fund-raising tool. For many, the term "prayer support" is a code word for financial support. "Send us a letter of encouragement and tell us you are praying for us" may well be saying between the lines, "Send us some money for our ministry."

We hardly notice the inconsistency of a Christian radio program closing with the words, "As you know, this is a venture of faith. We are looking to God alone to meet all our needs, as you His people give generously to support this effort, which reaches millions of needy people with the gospel. Our program costs $50,000 each week. Please write and encourage us. Your letters mean much. We would like to send you at no charge a booklet entitled . . ."

Of course there is nothing wrong with asking for money. But it is inconsistent to profess that the ministry is living by faith in God alone while at the same time an overt advertising strategy is being employed.

Many are discovering that religion pays. We can get Jesus T-shirts, pencils, and even candy with scriptural verses on the wrapper.

Not only is God's house of prayer being used to make money, but also the masses are being told that prayer can make them rich. I was watching a Christian entrepreneur appeal for funds in order to build a high-rise office/television studio building. He assured his viewers that they could get a thirtyfold increase if they would pray, a sixtyfold increase if they would pray and give, and a hundredfold increase if they would pray, give, and fast.

Prayer is being touted as a way to get what you want. Today there are faith preachers, faith teachers, faith movements, even faith churches. It is being taught that faith isn't about asking God for what you need; it is about asking Him for what you dream of. They are saying, "If you can dream it, you can have it."

People are being urged to pray, "Lord, bless me, prosper me, and give me." Some of these teachers argue that Jesus must have dressed in designer clothes. Why else would the soldiers have wanted His garments!

The Scriptures foretold our day: "This know also, that in the last days perilous times shall come. For men shall be lovers of their own selves, covetous, boasters, proud, blasphemers, disobedient to parents" (2 Timothy 3:1, 2).

In order to be user-friendly, in some quarters modern religious teachers have tailor-made a gospel that instead of calling for self-denial is actually cut to the size of those who love themselves and are covetous. To those who love money, instead of calling for self-denial, the message is that when properly applied with just the right amount of faith, prayer can actually help you get more money than ever.

Have we once again converted a house of prayer into a marketplace?

Our prayers reflect what is important to us. If our goals are materialistic, this will be reflected in our prayers. In Matthew 6 Jesus tells us not to make material things our first concern. He says not to worry about the flesh and its support groups, but He admonishes us to seek first the kingdom of God and His righteousness. (Do a self-audit of your last 10 prayers. If you are like many people, they probably were mostly about what Jesus told us not to worry about!)

If material prosperity in this life is promised for God's children, then our prayers become a cruel joke. Most of the people on this planet are poor. There are at least a billion people who earn less than $400 per year. During my ministry I have seen the grinding poverty of the masses, but among those masses I have also seen giants of faith. To me this did not come as a surprise. When the early church was being established, the apostle James wrote, "Hearken, my beloved brethren, Hath not God chosen the poor of this world rich in faith, and heirs of the kingdom which he hath promised to them that love him?" (James 2:5).

Contrary to what is being taught by some, Jesus was not a rich man. He owned no property (Luke 9:58). Though He was poor, He was not against the rich. Jesus did not teach that riches are evil, but He did remind His listeners that riches are dangerous. "Again I tell you, it is easier for a camel to go through the eye of a needle than for a rich man to enter the kingdom of God" (Matthew 19:24, RSV).

Prosperity is not evil. "The diligent man will get precious wealth" (Proverbs 12:27, RSV). "A good man leaves an inheritance to his children's children" (Proverbs 13:22, RSV). "The soul of the diligent is richly supplied" (verse 4, RSV).

Yet Jesus warns us that we cannot serve two masters. He doesn't teach that we must balance the material with the spiritual; He says that we must put spiritual things first. "Lay not up for yourselves treasures upon earth, where moth and rust doth corrupt, and where thieves break through and steal: but lay up for yourselves treasures in heaven, where neither moth nor rust doth corrupt, and where thieves do not break through nor steal: for where your treasure is, there will your heart be also" (Matthew 6:19-21).

We can transfer money from bank to bank, but we cannot transfer money to heaven. When Jesus tells us to lay up treasure in heaven, He is not so much asking us to give money to charity as He is asking us to have a spiritual rather than a materialistic perspective on life.

The story of the rich young ruler is a sad one. "Then Jesus beholding him loved him, and said unto him, One thing thou lackest: go thy way, sell whatsoever thou hast, and give to the poor, and thou shalt have treasure in heaven: and come, take up the cross, and follow me' " (Mark 10:21). Jesus was not telling the young man what he had to do in order to follow Him. He simply was asking, "If you had to choose Me or money, which would it be?" The young man wanted it both ways.

The life of Jesus was one of service. As long as Jesus was serving the people, healing the sick, raising the dead, casting out demons, or feeding the thousands, there were crowds to follow Him. But when He stood up that day in the Temple and called for a heart commitment on the part of His listeners, they in effect said, "We're outta here."

During World War II the Allies in the Pacific theater used little islands that up to that time were almost unheard-of as supply bases for the armies as they skipped across the Pacific. The islanders who had never before seen civilization, suddenly saw the sky filled with flying machines that brought races of people they had never seen. These gods from the sky brought jeeps, refrigerators, Zippo lighters, fans, and weapons. They constructed buildings, control towers, and airfields.

Then, as abruptly as they had come, they left. The islanders were amazed. They assumed that these people were from heaven. As a result, the local peoples developed a new religion called the cargo religion—the cargo, of course, being the things the people from the sky had brought. The cargo cults taught that someday in the future the cargo gods would return, and so to be ready they built models of airplanes and control towers from rods and bamboo—all in preparation for the second coming of the cargo gods.

Not long afterward the missionaries came to the islands. At first the members of the cargo cults received them gladly, thinking that this was the second coming of the cargo gods. The missionaries, of course, had come to preach the gospel, but when the local people saw that there was no cargo accompanying the message, they soon lost interest in what the missionaries were trying to do.

Cargo cults are believed to be a reaction to the materialism of Caucasian culture that pervaded Melanesia during the past century.

They all share a millennium belief that a mysterious ship or plane will arrive to bring enough food and goods so that people will no longer have to work.

We must be on guard in this materialistic culture so that we do not also develop our own cargo cult. Jesus has told us that the important things in a person's life are not their material possessions. "And he said unto them, Take heed, and beware of covetousness: for a man's life consisteth not in the abundance of the things which he possesseth" (Luke 12:15).

This generation is teaching the opposite to the point that it measures the blessing of God with a material yardstick. Religious people are driving fine cars, wearing designer clothes, and living in expensive houses, which they claim were given to them by God as an answer to their prayers. Faith and prayer are seen as a way to do "insider trading" with God. Persons in this camp would be among those run out of the Temple when Jesus said, "You have made My house of prayer a den of thieves."

The model prayer takes us back to basics. It references our material needs in a simple way. "Give us this day our daily bread" (Matthew 6:11). This perspective will not put stress on Jesus' command to us to seek first the kingdom of heaven and His righteousness.

It is interesting to note that the everyday building materials of heaven are gold and precious stones. When the streets are pure gold and the gates are of pearl, these commodities have been effectively devalued in the heavenly economy. There is the well-known parable of the man who tried to enter heaven carrying a suitcaseful of the gold that he had accumulated while on this earth. He informed the angel at the gate that he would not be happy in heaven unless he could bring along his wealth.

The angel told the man he'd see what he could do. When asked by the angel in charge what the man wanted to bring in, the gate angel shrugged his shoulders and replied, "Pavement."

Our prayers must not be allowed to degenerate to the level of pavement. Though we may pray for that which is necessary to sustain us, the prayer of our heart should be for the true riches that are in our Lord Jesus Christ.

"O the depth of the riches both of the wisdom and knowledge of God! how unsearchable are his judgments, and his ways past finding out!" (Romans 11:33).

"That in the ages to come he might shew the exceeding riches of his grace in his kindness toward us through Christ Jesus" (Ephesians 2:7).

It is interesting that often after receiving the offering, a congregation will stand and sing, "Praise God, from whom all blessings flow." The implication is obvious: "Blessings" are usually about money. If having a lot of money is proof of the blessing of God, then the Mafia must be doing something right!

This chapter is not meant to be a condemnation of those who have material wealth, but it is, in the words of the apostle Paul, a challenge to arrange our priorities. "Charge them that are rich in this world, that they be not highminded, nor trust in uncertain riches, but in the living God, who giveth us richly all things to enjoy" (1 Timothy 6:17).

The time is upon us when all that is the riches of this world will come to nothing. "For in one hour so great riches is come to naught. And every shipmaster, and all the company in ships, and sailors, and as many as trade by sea, stood afar off. . . . And they cast dust on their heads, and cried, weeping and wailing, saying, Alas, alas, that great city, wherein were made rich all that had ships in the sea by reason of her costliness! for in one hour is she made desolate" (Revelation 18:17-19).

This is no time to pray, "God, make me rich," but time to deny ourselves, take up our cross, and follow the one who gave everything for us. We are strangers and pilgrims here. This earth is not our home. We are just passing through. Our treasures are laid up somewhere beyond the blue. Whether we be poor in this world's goods or have more than enough, as children of God in every economic group the focus of our prayer should be that of Moses, who esteemed "the reproach of Christ greater riches than the treasures in

IF WITH ALL YOUR HEART

Egypt: for he had respect unto the recompence of the reward" (Hebrews 11:26).

Points to Consider
1. A selfish heart will pray from selfish motives.
2. The purpose of prayer must not be to lay up treasures on this earth but rather treasure in heaven.

Some Things to Pray About
1. That the Lord will forgive us when we seek first the things of this earth rather than things that have eternal value.
2. That God will be especially close to the poor of this world who are rich in faith.

CHAPTER 14

STRENGTH IN NUMBERS

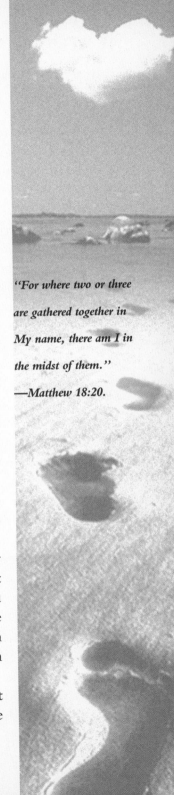

There is no doubt: There is strength in numbers when it comes to prayer. But does it take a lot of people praying to convince God to do the right thing? In this chapter we will consider the benefits of praying together and in what ways there is strength in numbers as far as prayer is concerned.

Although religion is a personal matter, it is not a private matter. The design of prayer is to develop not only a private one-on-one relationship with God but also fellowship with each other.

Ultimately prayer is to bring us into unity. Jesus prayed before He led His disciples to Gethsemane, "that they all may be one; as thou, Father, art in me, and I in thee, that they also may be one in us: that the world may believe that thou hast sent me. And the glory which thou gavest me I have given them; that they may be one, even as we are one: I in them, and thou in me, that they may be made perfect in one" (John 17:21-23).

It was the last day of the Week of Prayer at the conference where I worked. Each day there

"For where two or three are gathered together in My name, there am I in the midst of them."
—Matthew 18:20.

had been a different speaker, and Friday's speaker was excellent. After she finished her homily, the leader asked if there were any requests for prayer. There were at least a dozen.

As I listened to the requests, it occurred to me that not one had anything to do with the sermon we had just heard. It was then for the first time that I began to wonder if, when we come together to pray, we are really praying together. Is it possible that, although we are together physically, we are not together in spirit and in purpose?

No doubt we each come to prayer with special concerns. There can be nothing wrong with sharing these burdens and asking others to pray with us, but is it not also important to set aside our personal cares for a time and pray for the needs we all share? It sounds ridiculous, but group prayer can easily become an occasion to think, *I'll pray for what you want if you'll pray for what I want.*

We live in a culture in which the focus is on me, myself, and mine. Of course we have differences, but it seems we have chosen to institutionalize them, to protect and emphasize these differences. In other words, we seem to have decided to focus on what makes us different rather than on what we have in common.

While our Creator made us different (when He finished me, He must have said, "I don't think I will do that again!"), the differences were to be compatible and complementary. From the beginning Satan's argument was that the unity of heaven, instead of bringing happiness, was inhibiting personal growth and self-realization and that there was more to be gained by doing your own thing than by working for the good of the whole.

In twenty-first-century society and even in the church there is an emphasis on diversity and what is called pluralism. This move is well intentioned as an attempt to unite us in our differences, but the result in many instances seems to be driving a wedge between generations, genders, races, and cultures.

Granted, we are different; yet like pieces of a puzzle fit together to form a big picture, so in the church and in the home we must see ourselves not as the only one who matters but as a part of a bigger picture—the family of God. Though we will never see eye to eye on all matters, we must come into unity in spite of our differences. And this can be done through the medium of prayer.

To be united in prayer does not exclude praying for each other's needs, but it must be dominated by praying for the common need. This can be an exciting concept, because thinking of what we all need is what unity is about. To be able to pray for a common need will by its very nature bring about reconciliation and have the effect of putting us all on the same level.

There is a danger, however, in using group prayer to try to manipulate and intimidate. Expressions such as "Help John to realize that I am right and he is wrong" are examples of praying *at* and not *with*. I have even caught myself praying at my grandchildren with words such as "Lord, please help Andrea to be a good girl and make her bed every morning." That might be all right as long as I add, "And forgive me for being impatient, and help me always to be kind."

In Matthew 18:19 Jesus says, "Again I say unto you, That if two of you shall agree on earth as touching any thing that they shall ask, it shall be done for them of my Father which is in heaven."

Of course, this is not saying that two or three people can outvote God. I have heard this promise taken quite literally. As they pray, a person might ask God for a particular thing, and someone in the group will add, "I agree with that, Lord." In all seriousness, this text is calling for more than someone seconding our motion.

As we will discuss more fully in the chapter, "Bite-sized Faith," prayer is much more than asking for something; it is a commitment to action. To agree with the prayer of another is to commit oneself to the purpose for which the request is being made.

Praying together will bring unity, and this unity must be expressed by the words we use. The past 20 years have seen a new kind of music called praise music. The pronouns used in this music are more often than not You (referring to God) and I (me).

One Sabbath morning a group of young adults was leading the congregation in singing praise songs whose words were projected on a large screen. When the singing was finished, I stepped to the platform and invited the singers to lead us in singing again the song we had just sung, but this time changing the words a little. Every time the word "I" was used, I suggested we sing "we," and each time the word "me" was used, we would sing "us." After all, this was a group song. The result was electrifying.

I invite you to try it sometime. You see, when we come together to worship, we come in the door as *I,* but once inside we are no longer I but *we* and *us*. How can 500 people sing praise to God at the same time in the same place using the pronoun "I"?

This concept is even more important when it comes to prayer. When we pray together we should use the pronoun "we" rather than "I." When Jesus taught us to pray, He said we should say, "Our Father." Why not "My Father"? The use of the word "our" precludes any thought of selfishness or exclusiveness. We are one family and we have one Father. When I pray alone, He is "my Father," but when we pray together, He is "our Father." When prayer is offered in a group setting, the use of "I" and "me" engenders a sense of exclusivity, as though the one praying has God's ear alone and the others are merely onlookers. Using the plural pronouns of "we" and "us" will include all worshipers in the prayer.

There is what might be called an occupational hazard of praying in public: Sometimes the prayer seems to be more for the public than for God. Prayer, both public and private, is no time to be self-conscious. We can put away flowery expressions and contrived words and speak to God from our hearts. We must be aware that the one to whom our prayer is being directed is not another person.

There are several ways to determine the focus of our public prayers. If I pray longer in public than I pray in secret, I'm probably praying to the public. If I'm more conscious of myself or of my surroundings than of the presence of God, I need to refocus my prayer. If I'm more concerned about the form of the words I use or of the opinions of others rather than of God, I'm missing the target of my prayer.

Sometimes when others are praying, we find ourselves not paying attention because we are planning what we are going to say next. It sounds ridiculous, but we often think how we should start our prayer with more colorful words. We wonder how we can put more action into our prayer and make it sound more spiritual. We want to word it differently from the person who is praying before us and make it sound more important and interesting. All this while the other person is praying.

Prayer is not to be a speech, but a conversation. Just as we can talk one on one with God, so it is possible for us to talk *together* with God. A private audience with an important person doesn't have the same dynamic as meeting with someone as a group. The group must not only agree with what they are each going to say, they must listen to each other so that what they say will be complementary and indicative of the unity of the group.

There are some who for one reason or another simply do not pray out loud in the presence of others. Granted, there are individuals who are shy even in conversing with friends. But in general it will do us good to learn to pray together. There are factors that may make it difficult for some to pray out loud:

1. There may be concern of what others will think. We may imagine that an inability to pray well in public will indicate that we are not spiritual or that we don't know how to pray. Some may also be concerned that if they pray out loud they will cry.

2. Some may resist praying in public because they are afraid of leaving a bad impression. Often public prayers are long and tiring to those who must listen. People often use clichés and seem to lack sincerity.

3. Some aren't comfortable praying in what for them is their second language. They feel that they don't know the language of prayer and that their prayers will sound "unlearned."

4. Others may find it difficult to pray in public because they find it difficult to be intimate with a God with whom they don't have a personal relationship.

IF WITH ALL YOUR HEART

It is common when praying in a group to assign certain ones to pray, to pray around the circle, or perhaps to ask for volunteers. In recent years a popular form of public prayer has been the "conversational prayer." In this type of prayer, a conversation with God is begun by a leader and continued by others on either an informal basis or as prearranged. An interesting characteristic of this type of group prayer is that the person who finishes praying doesn't say "Amen"; rather, someone else will join in the prayer and continue the "conversation." Not only that, but those in the group may pray as often as they like. The leader will usually close and give the amen.

A conversational prayer is just that. It is not a speech but a conversation. Some important points about conversational prayer are:

1. In conversational prayer we are truly praying together and will therefore be aware of those around us—their rights, privileges, and feelings. Conversational prayer is a group effort.

2. Good conversation implies that we must take turns and do it gracefully. When one person does all the talking, we call it a monologue. That isn't conversation.

3. In conversational prayer we endeavor to pursue the same subject or at least make reference to it before changing the topic. In conversations with each other, we try to be gracious when we change the subject. We should do likewise in conversational prayer.

4. In a conversation each person must use their memory to recall, their patience to wait, their alertness to jump in, and their willingness to get out. In other words, they must be in tune with what is going on.

5. A conversational prayer will probably last much longer than we are accustomed to praying individually. For this reason, those who participate may choose to kneel or sit rather than stand. There is no specific posture for this kind of praying, but it should be comfortable and of course respectful, keeping in mind the age and physical condition of each participant.

At a time in which there is disunity all around us, we can be united through the medium of prayer. When rightly understood, periods of prayer together can be unforgettable experiences and occasions that will cement our relationship with God and with each other.

After Jesus had returned to heaven, the disciples and others came together to pray. Scripture says, "And when the day of Pentecost was fully come, they were all with one accord in one place" (Acts 2:1).

It is not enough that we come together to pray; we must also be of one accord. Once when I was on an airplane, a pilot was seated next to me. He was returning home from a tour of duty. We talked, of course, about airplanes. In the course of the conversation he said that a passenger airliner is comprised of some 2 million pieces flying together in close formation!

I have never forgotten that analogy. In the church we are comprised, as it were, of many "different pieces," but as we fly along toward our heavenly destination we must be joined together in close formation. Understanding the significance and true meaning of prayer will make this possible.

Often there are problems in the church, differences of opinion that instead of being resolved become a serious impediment to the overall well-being of the church. When we have problems among ourselves, be they in the church or in the family, one of the first things that seems to happen is that we stop praying together. When we are not praying together, what would otherwise be resolvable molehills may well become mountains that separate us and keep us from working together. Worse still, they keep God from being able to work through us.

Is there strength in numbers? The answer is yes and no. No in the sense that God is our strength and He is our majority. Yes because God manifests His strength through His body on earth, the church. It is through prayer that in spite of our differences we become united with Him. The closer you get to God in prayer, and the closer I get to God in prayer, the closer we become with each other and the more powerful will be the Holy Spirit as He works in us both to do His good pleasure.

IF WITH ALL YOUR HEART

Points to Consider
1. Praying together is more than being in the same place at the same time.
2. Though we have specific needs, we have many needs in common and should identify and pray about these needs when we come together in Jesus' name.

Some Things to Pray About
1. That the Lord will help me to think of the needs of others and not only of my own.
2. That the Lord will help me to think in terms of *us*, not just *me*.

CHAPTER 15

BITE-SIZED FAITH

I f you were to stop praying today, would it make any difference in your life? Or would you be able to carry on grandfathered in by the prayers of others? How important to your day-by-day existence are your prayers?

"Ridiculous questions," you may reply. "I couldn't live if I didn't pray."

Another question, then. What are you praying about? The reason I ask is that prayer can easily become a routine to which little or no thought is given, much like sending in the reply card that promises some type of drawing. If we are lucky, which we know we won't be, we will win; but if not, no matter, we will go on with our lives.

While we are asking ourselves some questions, let me pose another: If we were about to pray together and your spouse or children were there, and if I were to ask them what you will say when you pray, could they tell me?

I had been invited to speak at a camp meeting in the Northeast. The conference president

"Ask, and it shall be given you; seek, and ye shall find; knock, and it shall be opened unto you."

—Luke 11:9.

had graciously assigned a pastor to each of the guest speakers. It was this pastor's task to call the speaker and have prayer for the ministry that the speaker would render at the coming encampment. One day I received such a call.

"Hello, I am Pastor So-and-so [he gave his name]. I have been asked by the president to pray for you as a speaker at camp meeting this year."

I was moved. We ministers often pray for others, but it is not so common that others will have a personal prayer for us. "Thank you," I replied. "I appreciate this very much."

We talked for a while. After about 10 minutes the pastor on the other end of the line said, "Do you mind if I pray for you now?" And he began to pray.

I appreciated his prayer very much; however, I still have to wonder about hearing him say, "Lord, help Pastor O'Ffill to tear up his notes and let the Spirit speak."

I remember wondering at the time, *Doesn't the Spirit speak to my heart when I am preparing my sermon? Does thinking out what I am going to say in advance mean that I am not speaking from my heart?*

It seems to me that it is important to consider beforehand what we are going to pray about.

From time to time my work requires me to go before ADCOM, the administrative committee of the conference in which I work. Before I go in, I am careful to prepare whatever documents are necessary so that the members of the committee will understand where I'm coming from. I will also spend time thinking about what I'm going to say and how I'll answer questions that may be asked me. The same should be true of prayer.

This brings up another question: Is it possible to pray without getting personally involved in helping God answer our prayers? Is prayer a process in which we simply send our requests winging their way up to heaven and then go about our way? Or is it reasonable, if not expected, that we should send along our prayers as we do registered mail: "Return Requested."

Life is real, and our prayers must be real. We make plans, and then we carry them out. When we ask God to do something, it's reasonable to make plans to be involved as He answers our requests. Our lives are both active and reactive. Our prayers should be the same.

On one occasion Jesus asked His listeners a question about construction. "For which of you, intending to build a tower, sitteth not down first, and counteth the cost, whether he have sufficient to finish it?" (Luke 14:28). Our Lord was a journeyman carpenter. If a customer asked Him to build something, Jesus knew the material, the tools, and the design required to fulfill the buyer's expectation.

When we pray, we should also count the cost. We should contemplate what would be necessary on our part for the Lord to answer our requests. It isn't difficult for our prayers to become vague and pointless. We tend to pray in broadbrush strokes and often don't give thought to the fine details that God may well bring together to do His will. Although God's ways are not our ways nor His thoughts our thoughts, if our prayers are to be effective we must at least try to see things from God's point of view. Someone once said that wisdom is seeing life from God's point of view, and knowledge is the ability to do what He would do in a particular situation.

I once received a call from a distraught father. He had raised his daughter in a Christian environment. He had given her a Christian education from grade school through college. Now she was on her own. Her first marriage had dissolved, and now she was living with a man who was not her husband.

Having done all in his power to assure that she would remain faithful to the church, he was frustrated to the point of being angry at what he concluded was a personal insult to his generosity. A well-known evangelist was about to hold evangelistic meetings in the city where his daughter lived. His question to me was "How can I persuade her to attend the meetings?"

I could understand his disappointment and frustration, but as we talked it became evident that there was more than just his daughter's salvation involved. His wife had continued to have a relationship with the daughter, but since the young woman was living with a man who was not her husband, the father had refused to visit her. His excuse was that he didn't want her to think he approved of what she was doing.

Now it was my turn to gently lead him to see the situation as it actually was. Although his concern for her spiritual well-being was completely understandable, his attitude had evidently become a stumbling block that would make it difficult for God to answer his prayers for his daughter's salvation.

I pointed out to him that, though it was a good idea that his daughter attend the upcoming meetings, there was a problem that needed to be resolved first—he needed to be reconciled with her. How could the Spirit convince her to come back to her heavenly Father when in practice her earthly father was rejecting her?

The issue for this man was not whether he should accept his daughter's living arrangement, but would he accept his daughter?

A few years ago I wrote a book titled *Lord, Keep Your Mansions—Just Save My Children*. In it I related some of the challenges that Betty and I have faced through the years. We had to cope with drug addiction and the sadness of divorce on the part of some of our children. Through it all it became apparent to us that if God was going to be able to answer our prayers for our children, it would not be *without* us but *with* us and at times *through* us.

It is my conviction that, though there are times we cannot solve a particular situation, we can always make matters worse.

When thinking of building a new house, we may decide to go to an architect. We tell them what we would like to see in a house, and they do a drawing and floor plan of the finished product. But before the house can be built there must be a detailed drawing that gives the dimensions of all the rooms, the walls, and the roof, plus the plumbing, the electricity, the trim, and all the rest. From this detailed blueprint a materials list is drawn up, and the project can be priced.

As we bring our requests to the Lord not only do we need to have an idea of what we would like for Him to do, but we should study His Word to know what answering that prayer will involve and what it will cost us personally.

Question: How do you eat an elephant? Answer: One bite at a time. Our faith must be big enough and bold enough to ask for great things, but in doing so we must employ bite-sized faith—a faith that can be applied one piece at a time.

"Bless my family" is a noble prayer, but what are we asking the Lord to do? If the Lord is going to bless our families, what will that look like and how can we cooperate with the Lord in making this possible?

Jesus said, "He that is faithful in that which is least is faithful also in much" (Luke 16:10). We often try to succeed in the big things—such as inviting a son or a daughter to attend an evangelistic meeting—while overlooking the personal relationships necessary to make that invitation credible.

Years ago we lived in a town in central Ohio. This was in the days before the large chain stores. There was one department store in the town, named after its owner. One day I was in the store and was surprised to see the owner standing behind one of the counters doing the work of a salesperson. I commented to him that it was interesting to see an important person such as himself out working on the floor of the store. I will never forget how he responded. "I make sure that I do the little things in life; and when I do, there are seldom any big things to do."

The story is told of a man in New York City who needed directions. He stopped a passerby and asked him how to get to Fifth Avenue. The person thought a moment and said, "Go straight ahead three blocks and turn left. No, don't do that, go to the second light and take a right. Keep going until you come to the next light. No, that is not the way. Go back about five blocks and hang a left, then . . . no, that is not it either. Come to think of it, you can't get there from here."

Our prayers should be big, but they can be so big that in a practical sense you can't get there from here. The next time we ask God to bless something, be it our family, the church, or some far-off mission field, we would do well to have thought out how God might do that.

One day Jesus said to His disciples, "The harvest truly is great, but the labourers are few: pray ye therefore the Lord of the harvest, that he would send forth labourers into his harvest" (Luke 10:2). It would have little meaning for us to pray this prayer unless we ourselves are willing to be one of the laborers.

A little girl and her family were having family worship one evening. One of the subjects of their prayers was a poor woman in the church. The little girl's daddy prayed that God would remember the poor woman and would provide for her needs. When the prayer was over, the little girl said, "Daddy, we have a lot of food. Why don't you answer that prayer yourself?" Though God works in mysterious ways, His ways usually include people, and that person might as well be you or me.

One day I was listening to a program in which Joni Eareckson Tada and her husband were being interviewed. They explained how, before they visit friends, they offer a prayer that God will give them the words to speak so that they might be a spiritual encouragement to the people.

When I heard them, my heart was touched. I am accustomed to praying before I make a pastoral visit or before going to a Bible study, but I hadn't thought about praying before going to visit friends. Betty and I live just a couple miles from one of our children and his family. I wonder what might happen if, before we jumped into the car to go visit the grandchildren, we prayed that God would help us to be a spiritual encouragement to the family by our attitude and by the words that we speak.

A commonly held pet peeve is receiving phone calls from telephone solicitors—telemarketers, we call them. The tendency is to hang up on them or otherwise not be polite. On several occasions I have deliberately entered into conversations with them. Often they are young people trying to earn their way through college. One young woman told me she makes 400 calls a day. When I hung up the phone, my heart was touched. I didn't feel so offended as I realized that she was a person like me just trying to make a living.

May I make a suggestion? The next time the phone rings during suppertime, before you answer you might consider a little prayer. It might go something like this: "Lord, help me to be kind."

As a postscript to this chapter, just as I had finished the last paragraph the phone rang. It was a person selling something. I took my own advice and said a little prayer. I even read to her what I had just written. Can you believe that? Aren't you glad that God isn't finished with us yet?

Points to Consider

1. Sometimes our prayers are so general we can't see the trees for the forest!
2. Have you considered what the cost will be to you if God uses you to answer your prayers?

Some Things to Pray About

1. That the Holy Spirit will impress us if there is something we are doing that keeps God from answering our prayers.
2. That we will always remember to be kind.

CHAPTER 16

TRUST
AND OBEY

*"Teach me to do thy
will; for thou art my
God: thy spirit is good;
lead me into the
land of uprightness."*
—Psalm 143:10.

Someone has said that if two angels were called to appear before the throne of the Almighty, and one were commanded to go and rule the earth's mightiest kingdom and the other were asked to be the garbage collector in a filthy village, both would be happy, because their joy is to do the will of God.

For more than 25 years I have made prayer a special study. I have come to the conclusion that when all is said and done, the purpose of prayer is ultimately not to get God to do our will, but rather it is to discover His and then to receive from Him the grace to do it. Put another way, the purpose of prayer is obedience.

In this next-to-the-last chapter of this book, the subject is obedience. It is important that we understand that prayer and obedience are intimately connected. A life of prayer is ultimately a pursuit of obedience.

The word "obedience" has fallen on hard times in recent years. We Christians have redis-covered the truth that we are saved by grace through faith. And now for many obedience is seen at worst as legalism or at best as merely another option for the Christian life.

I have heard a gospel invitation that goes something like this: "Now that you have salvation, won't you accept Jesus as the Lord of your life?" Translated, that means "Now that you have been saved, won't you please consider obeying Jesus?"

There can be no doubt that love is the basis of our relationship with Jesus, and this love will be expressed by obedience to His will.

Which is most important, then, to a person's redemption: to reestablish love or reestablish obedience? The fact is that they cannot be separated. Love cannot exist in those whom God has created without expressing itself in obedience; and by the same token true obedience cannot exist without love.

When I reference obedience I am talking about obedience as an *attitude,* not merely something a person does. This is because a person can appear on the outside to be obedient, yet in reality be a rebel and a traitor.

It may come as a shock to some, but disobedience is actually unforgivable. You see, if God tolerated disobedience in any form, at any time, the result would be anarchy. God does not tolerate disobedience. Neither does He negotiate with it. He is, however, merciful to the disobedient—for the time being. However, as we know from what happened before the Flood, His spirit will not always "strive with man" (Genesis 6:3).

Disobedience lies at the root of all sin and misery. The goal of salvation must be to cut away this root of sin and return us to our original destiny—that is, to return us to a life of obedience.

Obedience was the condition for living in the Eden paradise. And, by the way, it is also the condition of those who will live in Paradise restored. Revelation 22:14 says, "Blessed are they that do his commandments, that they may have right to the tree of life."

Obedience is a dominant theme in both the Old and New Testaments. Paul says that he was commissioned to make Gentiles obedient (Romans 15:18).

IF WITH ALL YOUR HEART

In James 1:22 we are called to be obedient, to be doers of the word and not hearers only.

First Peter 1:2 declares that the sanctification wrought by the Holy Spirit leads us to obedience. Verses 14 and 15 call us to reject our former lives and be obedient.

Noah's obedience is mentioned four times in Genesis.

God said to Israel in Exodus 19:5, "If ye will obey my voice indeed, . . . then ye shall be a peculiar treasure unto me above all people."

It must be understood by us freethinking, independent, open-minded citizens of the twenty-first century that we are God's people only if we obey Him. "Obey my voice and I will be your God" (Jeremiah 7:23). The blessings and cursings recorded in Deuteronomy 11:26-28 revolve around obedience.

Obedience to His Father was the theme of Jesus' life on earth. He referred to obedience in a wonderful way. He said, "Father, I want to do what You want Me to do" (see Hebrews 10:9). In another verse Jesus said, "I seek not mine own will, but the will of the Father" (John 5:30).

Obedience is the mark of the Spirit-filled life. The Holy Spirit is given to those who obey (Acts 5:32). This being true, a person who is knowingly and habitually disobedient does not and indeed cannot have the Holy Spirit.

The Old and the New Testaments from Genesis to Revelation proclaim the relationship between redemption and obedience. Paradise, Calvary, and Heaven itself all proclaim that the first and last thing God asks us is simply universal, unchanging obedience.

Though the gospel makes a provision for disobedience, salvation is not about how to disobey and get away with it, but how to be restored to a relationship of obedience to God and how to maintain that relationship.

Obedience is a characteristic of those who love God and is the starting point of true holiness. "Seeing ye have purified your souls in obeying the truth through the Spirit unto unfeigned love of the brethren, see that ye love one another with a pure heart fervently"

(1 Peter 1:22). Obedience is a mark of a true Christian.

A person who says they know Jesus and is knowingly disobedient is not telling the truth (1 John 2:4). Words are cheap. A person can claim to be anything, but as Grandma used to say, "The proof of the pudding is in the eating." The proof of love is always obedience—there is never an exception to this rule.

First John 3:18 tells us that love must be in "deed."

First John 5:3 says, "This is the love of God, that we keep His commandments."

It is clear that seeking to know God's will and doing it is what the Christian life is all about, and so this must ultimately be the goal of our prayers.

Now listen, people who say they have received Christ as their Savior and yet continue to knowingly disobey have, in fact, not really received Christ as their Savior at all. Because when Jesus Christ forgives us, He also gives us the Spirit of obedience. Obedience is the only way we can maintain our relationship to God and His righteousness.

The single, supreme, all-controlling power of Jesus' life was His obedience to His Father. A person may say, "But Jesus obeyed for us," or, "It is impossible for us to obey God." But Jesus said that obedience is a family trait of those who belong to His family. He said that His brothers and sisters are those who do the will of His Father (see Matthew 12:50).

Can a person carry obedience to God too far? Definitely not! Scripture says, "He that is faithful in that which is least is faithful also in much" (Luke 16:10). This is because the whole is the sum of its parts. The person who is obedient in little things is obedient, period. The person who is disobedient in little things is simply disobedient.

Perhaps you may be discouraged with all of this and say, "But everyone I know is disobedient in some way, including me."

Will disobedient people be saved? In an objective sense, yes. In a subjective sense, no. Let me explain. God will save people who lived up to all the light they had. But He cannot save those who were knowingly disobedient. A person who is persistently disobedient is actually fighting against what Jesus is trying to do in their life, because having Jesus in the life always brings with it a desire to obey.

It may be said that unless we really love God we cannot keep His commandments. But the reverse is also true, and that is, unless it is our purpose to keep His commandments, we'll never know what it's like to truly love God. Ultimately, love is not identified by what it is—that is a mystery. But love can always be identified by what it does—it always obeys according to the knowledge it has.

Thousands of sermons have been preached and nearly whole libraries have been written trying to show the relationship of faith to obedience.

To say we are saved by faith and not by obedience is true. At no time since sin came into the world was it ever possible to be saved by obedience. Obedience was never a *how;* it was always a *what.* We must stop talking about obedience when we are discussing how to be saved and rather talk about obedience in relationship to what salvation brings to the life of the Christian.

A person whose salvation is based on faith in Jesus Christ as their Savior will receive from Christ, by faith in this life, two things: (1) forgiveness from sin, and (2) an attitude or desire to obey.

This is what salvation is and does, and it's all a result of faith in Jesus.

There are some who would say that obedience is our response to Jesus' love. But think about it for a moment. Obedience is not something I give God, but rather something He gives to me. Obedience is just as much a gift of God as is forgiveness of sin. Is forgiveness His part and obedience our part? No. *All* that is our salvation is to the praise and glory of Jesus Christ, our Savior and our God!

Faith and obedience have the same relationship that the atria and the ventricles have in the heart—they are inseparable. They never can work independently of each other in the true sense. A forgiven person will always pray to be obedient.

In trying to separate faith and obedience, some have done what Solomon suggested be done with the surviving baby of the two mothers; that is, they have tried to cut the gospel in two.

As God formed the first human being of the dust of the earth and breathed into his nostrils the breath of life and he became a living soul, so justification and obedience are the living soul of what we call salvation—and both come by faith. When Jesus justifies a person, He sanctifies them; that is, He gives the gift of obedience. He never does one and not the other.

A young boy got hold of a big black cigar. He headed into a back alley where no one would see him, and lit it. It didn't taste good, but it made him feel very grown-up until he saw his father coming. The young man quickly put the cigar behind his back and tried to be as casual as possible. Father and son exchanged pleasantries for a moment. Then, trying to divert his father's attention in any way possible, the boy noticed a billboard nearby advertising the circus.

"Can I go, Dad?" he pleaded. "Can I go to the circus when it comes to town? Please, Dad?"

His father's reply was one that his son never forgot, and we would do well to remember it too.

"Son," he answered quietly but firmly, "one of the first lessons you need to learn about life is this: Never make a petition while at the same time trying to hide a smoldering disobedience behind your back."

Friend, if you and I are going to have effective heart-to-heart communication with our heavenly Father, we must first ask God to cleanse our hearts of any smoldering disobedience that we may be trying to hide.

Being knowingly disobedient to God's obvious will for our lives will ultimately crowd out prayer and in the meantime will make us a hypocrite, which, by the way, is the Greek word for "actor."

Contrary to what some may have thought, obedience to the will of God from the heart is not legalism. It is a wonderful gift that God gives to those who have accepted Jesus as their Lord and Savior.

Obedience brings with it great rewards, not only in this life, but in the life to come. "Blessed are they that do his commandments [his will], that they may have right to the tree of life, and may enter in through the gates into the city" (Revelation 22:14).

IF WITH ALL YOUR HEART

Points to Consider

1. Obedience didn't put Adam and Eve into the Garden of Eden, but it was disobedience that took them out.
2. A person who is born again will have a desire to do the will of God.

Some Things to Pray About

1. That the Holy Spirit will give us victory over any "smoldering" disobedience that may exist in our lives.
2. That we will be obedient to the will of God in every detail of our lives.

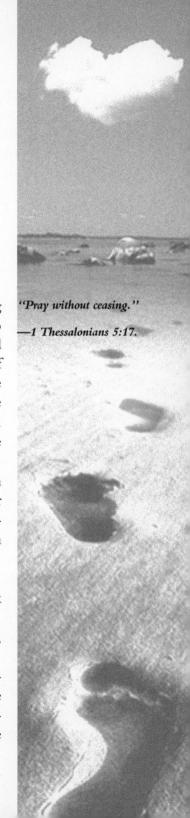

CHAPTER 17

PRAYER AS
A LIFESTYLE

O ne day a friend and I were discussing the matter of prayer. He related to me that he and his wife had attended a retreat for married couples. One of the purposes of the retreat was to encourage the spouses to communicate with each other. At one point they were asked to write each other notes. He told me that in one of his wife's notes she asked, "When do you pray?"

"Pray without ceasing."

—1 Thessalonians 5:17.

He was a minister. I am sure that her question was not inquiring when he prayed in church, or when he prayed with the children in family worship or before a meal. She wanted to know when he spent time alone with God.

"What did you tell her?" I asked.

He said, "I told her that I pray when I walk and I pray when I drive."

Then looking me right in the eye, he said, "Dick, I don't have time to pray."

I have never forgotten his words. His answer to his wife could make it appear that he was praying all the time, but in fact he was confessing to me that though he prayed "all the time," in reality he wasn't giving God any special time.

This chapter will bring out the fact that prayer is more than the time we spend alone with God. As we have learned throughout the book, prayer is more than the words we say to God. However, it would be a mistake to conclude that it is not necessary to spend special undivided time with God. And experience has taught us that the best time to spend with God is first thing in the morning.

When I told someone that I was going to write another book in which I would return to the subject of prayer, they guessed that it would include something about praying in the morning. They shared their hope that I would give practical suggestions for the benefit of those who are not morning people.

While it may be inspiring, it can also be intimidating to hear someone tell how they get up at 4:00 in the morning and pray for two hours. It can make one feel that anybody who is anybody spiritually has to get up before dawn, and if they don't, they must be a spiritual lesser life form.

To be able to say you have a devotional life has become the gold standard of the Christian life. While this goal can be an inspiration to some, when flaunted it often becomes a discouragement to others. Jesus left no room for doubt that devotional time was to be not only private but also secret. It must not be held up before others as a type of spiritual badge of courage.

To the individual who is not a morning person, and there are many, I would say (and I don't think I am contradicting what I have already said), that if you can't get up at 4:00 and spend some quality time with God, then spend some quality time with Him whenever you get up. This will not be to "be seen of men" (Matthew 6:5), but to survive. Starting the day (whenever you start your day) without committing your ways to the Lord can easily contribute to complicating your life further down the line.

Though I ate, drank, and breathed yesterday, my physical well-being—yes, my very existence—demands that I do the same every day. And so it is in our spiritual life. As a car cannot go far when the tank is on empty, so those whose spiritual life is on empty will soon find their relationship with Jesus stalled.

While it is essential to spend quality time with God each day, like everything else the devotional life can easily become a routine that not only loses meaning, but can even become unhitched from the rest of our lives.

One time I was saddened to learn that an acquaintance of mine decided he didn't love his spouse anymore. He apparently became infatuated with another woman. This is not unheard-of. But in this case the individual was very spiritual and even had the custom of getting up early in the morning to pray with others before beginning the tasks of the day.

When I heard what had happened in his life, I wondered how a person could get up early in the morning and spend time with God and at the same time watch their relationship with their spouse come apart.

If there is ever a time in which it is appropriate to hang out dirty laundry, it's in the time we spend alone with God, because "He that covereth his sins shall not prosper: but whoso confesseth and forsaketh them shall have mercy" (Proverbs 28:13). Only God knows the heart, but in this case the person may have been either too ashamed to talk to the Lord about what was going on in his life, or he had decided that the time he was spending in his devotional life was really all that mattered to the Lord.

When we pray we might as well be up front with the Lord. "For there is nothing hid, which shall not be manifested; neither was any thing kept secret, but that it should come abroad" (Mark 4:22).

I realized that this could happen to any of us when we compartmentalize our lives. Prayer was never meant to be an end in itself or simply another event in our daily lives. Prayer is a means to an end; it enables us to live holy lives.

In the seventeenth century there was a Frenchman known as Nicholas Herman of Lorraine. As a young man he was a soldier, but later he became a monk. We remember him as Brother Lawrence, and his contribution to our lives is that he has inspired us to practice the presence of God. With Brother Lawrence, his set times for prayer were not different from other times. For him prayer became a lifestyle.

I have been married to my wife for more than 40 years. The commitment Betty and I have to each other not only impacts our relationship, but affects all that we do.

While it goes without saying that marriages in which there is little or no communication are at risk, it's not necessary that I be talking with my wife continually. Our communion is more than words; it's a lifestyle. And so it is with our commitment to Jesus. Our lives must go beyond our prayers to our deeds. It is not enough just to talk to Him; we must live for Him.

Surveys have been conducted asking people if they pray. The results are both encouraging and discouraging. While the majority of the people interviewed said that they pray, most of them every day, prayer has little effect on the direction their lives are taking.

Many people have divided their lives into two compartments. They have what they see as a spiritual life and a secular life. A person who tries to maintain a balance between the spiritual and the secular could be compared to the image of Daniel 2, whose feet were made of iron and of clay. The prophet Daniel put it plainly: "They shall not cleave one to another" (Daniel 2:43). Our lives cannot be spiritual and at the same time secular. They are either one or the other.

A truly spiritual life will be one that not only begins the day with God but also includes the walk with Him all day. A true Christian's devotional life becomes a lifestyle—a practical demonstration of the text that says, "In him we live, and move, and have our being" (Acts 17:28).

We who are parents and grandparents carry huge burdens for the salvation of our loved ones. Every day, sometimes in tears, we hold them up before the Lord in prayer. Perhaps the first person we should bring before the Lord in prayer is ourselves. This is not to say that our prayers should be self-centered, but it is incompatible with the spirit of prayer to ask the Lord to change everything and everybody but ourselves.

You may say, "But Pastor O'Ffill, you don't understand. I am the way I am because of my wife. How can I have a changed life unless the Lord changes her?"

My answer is that you and I can have a changed life whether our wife or husband changes or not. I have seen many cases in which wives and husbands have had to pray for a spouse sometimes for years before there was a change. But the most important change of all had happened many years before, and that was when the Lord changed them.

There seem to be people who can tell so many stories of answered prayer that sometimes one is tempted to wonder why this always happens to them and not to us. But not to worry—a lifestyle of prayer always has a story, and that will be the story of the change in our own lives. Jesus challenges us as He did the man He healed at Gadara: "Go and tell what the Lord has done for you" (see Luke 8:39).

Several years ago my wife and I remodeled our kitchen. Part of the project was repainting the walls. To make the room another color it was not necessary to remove the old paint. We simply filled in the nail holes, sanded the surface a bit, and then put on the new coat of paint.

In the Christian life this is not possible. The new life in Christ is not something applied over the old life. "Therefore if any man be in Christ, he is a new creature: old things are passed away; behold, all things are become new" (2 Corinthians 5:17). I am convinced that the most important aspect of our personal prayer life is repentance. Jesus promised that He would send the Holy Spirit, and the first thing you would notice when He came is that you would be convicted of sin. "And when he [the Holy Spirit] is come, he will reprove the world of sin, and of righteousness" (John 16:8).

Our prayers must begin with a spirit of repentance, because repentance is about change, and change is what the gospel brings to our lives.

IF WITH ALL YOUR HEART

For some prayer has become a technique. I just finished reading a book whose premise is that if we really want God to answer our prayers we must *pray out loud*. The author said that if we would pray out loud with all our hearts, God would do wonderful things in our lives. He shared many stories of answers to prayer that illustrated his point. As I read I smiled. It occurred to me that it was not the praying out loud that brought the answers to prayers (the Pharisees prayed out loud), but rather the praying from the heart that touched the heart of God.

Indeed, there are blessings to be had by fasting, by praying all night, and by spending two hours every morning in prayer. But a person could conceivably do all of these things and not have their heart in it. Scripture warns that it is possible to have a form of godliness but deny the power thereof (2 Timothy 3:5). The final test of effective prayer is the changed life. Jesus puts it another way: "Wherefore by their fruits ye shall know them" (Matthew 7:20).

Prayer is not our idea. It is Jesus' initiative. He says, "Behold, I stand at the door [our heart], and knock: if any man hear my voice, and open the door [my heart], I will come in to him, and will sup with him, and he with me" (Revelation 3:20). Our relationship becomes a lifestyle.

Prayer is a subjective experience. Therefore, we would do well to remind ourselves that prayer could be so subjective that we can actually end up praying for the wrong things, or we can even be praying for the right things for the wrong reasons. "For we know not what we should pray for as we ought" (Romans 8:26).

For this reason we must continually turn to the Word of God in order to set the terms of reference for our prayers. While it is the Holy Spirit who knocks at the door of our hearts, calling us to pray, the Bible must always be our textbook, teaching us what we should pray about. To pray outside the framework of Scripture is to open oneself to the possibility that the devil may answer our prayers.

Friend, we have come to the end of this book. No book can possibly say all that can be said about prayer. It is as high as the heavens and as deep as the sea. This volume was written with the desire that our prayers (our words) will spring from our hearts and that this heart cry to our heavenly Father will be, through the power of the Holy Spirit, transformed into the most eloquent prayer of all—a holy life.

Points to Consider
1. The Christian life does not have a secular component.
2. While prayer is tailor-made for every circumstance, the measure of our prayers must always be taken by the Word of God.

Some Things to Pray About
1. That we will not hide anything from God.
2. That the Holy Spirit will give us an ongoing spirit of repentance.